Eleventh Hour in 2020 America

How America's foreign policy got jacked up – and how the next administration can fix it

By Lt. Col. Daniel L. Davis, USA, ret

Table of Contents

Preface

This book lays out compelling evidence that U.S. foreign policy for more than two decades has been an unqualified failure. If substantive changes are not made — soon — in how we engage with the world we risk suffering catastrophic loss.

Some may consider that an alarmist view and suggest that while we could do a better job in some areas, it's a stretch to suggest the risk of failure is that high. It is precisely because such views are so prevalent that I have been inspired to write this book: the stakes *are* that high, and the risk of failure *is* that real.

Whether Donald Trump wins a second term in November or Joe Biden is voted into office, it will be crucial that the country's jacked-up foreign policy be brought into conformity with new and emerging realities. If we continue the status quo of our current bipartisan foreign policy that has dominated for decades, we risk international obsolescence – or we'll fumble our way into an entirely avoidable, unnecessary, and pointless war.

This book points out our most prominent failures while highlighting the increasing risk we face in several corners of the globe. Many aspects of our foreign policy need to be corrected but some are more critical than others and need immediate triage.

As a career Army officer, I've studied those key areas in considerable detail and gained first-hand experience on the ground during four combat deployments. With that insight, I provide a vision for a new foreign policy that has a real chance of success, based on the current realities in the world (both positive and negative). It's a vision that the next administration – either Republican or Democrat – could choose to enact, to our collective benefit. I sincerely hope November's winner seizes that opportunity.

My great fear, however, is that the next Administration will be only incrementally different from all the other post-9/11 administrations.

What I *expect* to happen, unfortunately, is that we will let this opportunity pass by without action. It seems probable we will continue down the status quo road, that we'll continue to pay a high price for avoidable failure, that we'll continue most or all of our on-going, "forever-wars," and that eventually, we'll stumble into a real war that gashes our ability to defend the country and will undercut our ability to prosper.

If what I fear does come to pass, whoever is in charge will blame their predecessors or some foreign power – or just claim we were victims. That will almost certainly be false. In all likelihood, stumbling into a major war will be a disaster of our own making and our own choosing. We have been consistently planting the seeds of that future disaster over the past three decades, and increasing evidence suggests sprouts are already visible above ground.

In the initial stages of a new war, it won't matter how we got into it or whose fault it was; we will reflexively rally 'round the flag, "support the troops" and fight to win it. At that point, no one will give the slightest consideration of our culpability, will not question whether our actions contributed to the conflict, and above all won't consider sealing off the disaster before it gets too deep.

As a nation, we will indignantly press for full victory. That's just who we are. It's our DNA.

In many ways, that indomitable spirit and relentless desire to win is a great asset and has played a major role in how we became a superpower. But taken too far, it also can be the engine of our downfall: pressing forward and attempting to doggedly pursue all-out victory in a war that we should never have fought could, perversely, lead to an unnecessary, avoidable defeat.

My hope in writing this book is to appeal to the intellect and logic of all Americans to take a hard look at our policies now, while there is still time to make changes, and before any disaster strikes.

There is still time. As of this writing, we are not at war with China, Russia, North Korea, or Iran. We have the strongest military with an unequaled ability to project power globally. The dollar is still the dominant global currency and we still have the most powerful economy on the planet. From this position of strength and power, we can change course on our foreign policy to slowly work off the negative consequences that have already accrued owing to past misdeeds, avoid any catastrophic outcomes in the present, and actually increase our power to ensure continued freedom and economic prosperity for generations to come.

All that is possible and realistic at this moment. It remains to be seen whether we'll seize this opportunity or condemn ourselves to plunge blindly forward into an avoidable disaster. This book is written to expose *how* our foreign policy got jacked up, *why* it has bombed, and explains how it *can be* successful well into the future.

The choice is ours. Generations of Americans will either thank us for the enlightened and wise choices we make in the coming months and years – or condemn us for failing to see the obvious truth; for blundering forward into preventable disaster.

Daniel L. Davis, Washington, DC, September 22, 2020

Introduction

Let's just bluntly say this right up front: American foreign policy is jacked up.

Since Sept. 11, 2001, it has devolved to the point that the face of U.S. diplomacy to the world is a series of forever-wars in which no combat deployments ever end; coercive measures against even major nuclear powers range from muscular military demonstrations to routine use of economic sanctions, even against our allies. The purported intent of these actions is to keep our country safe and to improve our economy.

Instead, we spend exorbitant amounts in blood and treasure to produce almost the opposite.

These actions not only fail their intended purposes, but they deteriorate our security and worsen our international relations. Perhaps even worse, our policies have had a disastrous effect on American servicemen and women: <u>thousands of them</u> have been killed, <u>tens of thousands</u> wounded, and <u>*hundreds of thousands*</u> who suffered traumatic brain injuries and post-traumatic stress disorder. More than <u>$6 trillion</u> of our tax dollars have been utterly wasted.

Think about that for a moment: we are *paying* a shockingly high price to manufacture a perpetually failing foreign policy.

America desperately needs to change how it conducts foreign policy and how it uses the military. Continuation of this perpetual failure, however, is not ordained. There are very practical ways in which we can make our country safer, stop wasting billions of dollars each year, and improve our relations with our friends *and* competitors. Step one, however, is in acknowledging we have a problem.

Continuing to blindly follow a status quo formed during the past 20-plus years will ensure the failures continue and deepen. Until we acknowledge what should be painfully obvious failures, there will be no chance to turn things around. I have been a first-hand witness to much of our military failure, and after having lived almost nine years of my life outside the United States, have witnessed many examples of our diplomatic failures as well.

The seeds of today's problems were planted, counterintuitively, in 1991 after the U.S. obliterated Saddam Hussein's massive Army during Operation Desert Storm and in 1992 when the USSR dissolved and ended the Cold War. At that time, we were the world's singularly dominant economic and military superpower. We could, quite literally, do no wrong—or more accurately, no one was powerful enough to tell us we were doing wrong.

Russia was the rump survivor of the Soviet Union and was in economic and military shambles. The Middle East cowered from our massive and technologically superior military. China was still an aspiring developing nation with an anemic economy, and our Western allies passively acquiesced to our every demand. The world of 1992 was radically different than the one of 1952 at the beginning of the Cold War—a perfect time to adjust our foreign policy to match new realities.

Instead, we found it much easier to ride the status quo and bask in our glory. The wisest course of action in 1992 would have been to take three to five years to conduct a comprehensive analysis of the new state of affairs in the world. We would have conducted years-long conversations with our allies and engaged in substantive diplomacy with Russia and China.

Based on all those actions, we could have created new institutions and formed new strategies based on the world that had emerged. Finally, we would have slowly transitioned into a new normal that would have solidified our position as the dominant world power, reduced the need to rely on a military-first foreign policy, and if handled well, strengthened our ability to prosper via expanded trade opportunities abroad.

Instead, we almost immediately designated the weakened Russia as an enemy and began aggressively expanding NATO toward their border. We gave little consideration to China beyond wanting to exploit its economic potential for our country. We did make meaningful drawdowns in the number of active-duty troops compared to the Cold War, but we still expanded the locations of service members stationed abroad. We also kept NATO structures unchanged, for instance, by continuing to underwrite the security of Europe with American troops and dollars.

It's sheer conjecture if we would have been able to change our military-first approach to global affairs because the world changed permanently on Sept. 11, 2001. The initial wound we suffered on that day proved to be only the tip of the iceberg and set us on a downward path that continues our decline to this day.

Americans were understandably afraid of the unknown and shadowy world of terrorists, and the government leaped in to provide security and stability. President Bush responded to the attacks in a forceful way that punished those he said were guilty of the attacks in Afghanistan. His initial orders were limited in scope, militarily attainable, and offered the opportunity to safely end the conflict by the summer of 2002. Instead, the president wasted that golden opportunity and took us down a darker path from which we have never recovered.

By spring 2002, the Taliban had been annihilated and were no longer a viable entity; al-Qaeda was deeply wounded and dispersed into impotent cells throughout the Middle East. Bush should have then acknowledged the objectives had been attained and withdrawn our military force, transitioning our Afghan mission to a State Department-led humanitarian and diplomatic enterprise. Instead, he refused to take the win and expanded the conflict in ways that still haunt us today.

First, instead of keeping the conflict limited to anti-terrorism operations, Bush unilaterally expanded the enemy list in his "Axis of Evil" speech in January 2002, expressly declaring the states of Iraq, Iran, and North Korea as enemies.

Second, instead of withdrawing from Afghanistan in 2002 as conditions warranted, <u>Bush </u>added almost 7,000 troops that year. Then, in a <u>2007 speech, he</u> expressly expanded the mission to include Afghan nation-building. These tasks were militarily unattainable, objectives that could never be realized.

Third, and worst of all, Bush took the U.S. into a 2003 land war with Iraq that was wholly unnecessary for U.S. security and based on, at best, thin weapons-of-mass destruction intelligence (and <u>intentionally manipulated</u> at worst). The results of these three mistakes were as predictable as they have been harmful to American interests.

Following Bush's Axis of Evil speech, <u>North Korea said</u> it regarded the speech as "little short of declaring war" and by December of that year had restarted its nuclear program and kicked out UN inspectors. Four years later, Pyongyang tested its <u>first nuclear weapon</u> and our relations with North Korea remain tense to this day.

Since Bush refused to withdraw from Afghanistan in 2002, every administration since has tried various strategies, varying troop levels from as low as 8,600 to as many as 100,000, yet never succeeded in winning the war or ending the conflict. Nearly 20 years after its beginning, the war continues aimlessly eating American lives, and we continue bleeding scores of billions each year.

President Obama initially withdrew the U.S. from Iraq as he promised during his campaign, but then gave in to the pressure of the Washington establishment when ISIS emerged in 2014 and quickly returned troops to Iraq, where they remain, also with no strategy or plan to ever end.

ISIS <u>posed a threat</u> to the regimes of Baghdad and Damascus, but none to the U.S.; we could have contained ISIS to the region and allowed Iraq and Syria to handle their problem without having deployed a single U.S. boot.

Early in his presidency, Obama listened to bad advice on Afghanistan from key officials and advisors such as Robert Gates, Hillary Clinton, and David Petraeus, who were in large part architects of our militarized foreign policy. The president had campaigned on winning the 'good war' in Afghanistan. As most presidents find out firsthand, there is a difference between being a candidate and Commander in Chief.

Obama had a chance to wind down the Afghan war in a way that would end the futility while still securing our population from terrorist threats. Instead, he listened to the architects and expanded the war to 140,000 U.S. and NATO troops, seeking militarily unattainable objectives — virtually guaranteeing the war would continue without resolution.

Moreover, continuing several bad precedents Bush had set, Obama expanded the use of legally dubious drone wars throughout the Middle East. These strikes often hit the wrong target and killed hundreds of innocent civilians during Obama's two terms. He exerted little diplomatic effort to resolve the disputes with North Korea and sat by passively as they continued to expand their nuclear and ballistic missile arsenals. Worse, he committed combat or support troops to Syria, Yemen, and Libya.

None of the Obama uses of force accomplished their stated objectives: our troops remain in Syria to this day, the Yemen civil war continues without resolution, and nine years after his intervention, Libya remains a festering wound of a civil war.

As the Obama administration wound down, Trump ran on a platform of ending forever-wars and ending regime-change policies. As of the publication of this book, Trump has chosen the path of least resistance: despite rhetoric to the contrary, he has essentially maintained the foreign policy status quo of the past 20 years.

Trump has twice launched missiles into Syria against regime targets, continues to retain troops on the ground there, has thus far refused to end the war in Afghanistan (though as of this writing there are rumors he is considering withdrawing all troops by November), and still hasn't withdrawn the combat troops from Iraq. Trump has added to the country's foreign policy headaches by choosing to escalate tensions with Russia and China.

He ordered the assassination of Iran's senior ranking general, withdrew from the Joint Comprehensive Plan of Action (JCPOA) negotiated by Obama, and has kept the U.S. and Iran tenuously balancing on the precipice of war.

Trump at first made progress on the North Korean issue, but after listening to the advice of hawkish advisors in February 2019 at Hanoi he rejected a deal with Kim Jong Un. Since then, there has been no progress and relations remain tense.

Most troubling, Trump has unleashed a negative campaign against China in which he has, in an attempt to get better trade deals for the U.S., engaged in a destructive trade war that has harmed relations and cost American farmers, manufacturers, and transportation firms more than it helped with China.

In reaction to the global pandemic of the coronavirus, Trump has chosen to conduct a scorched earth foreign policy with Beijing that could one day spark a military conflict with the nuclear power. Trump's performance abroad has been largely consistent with every president since 9/11, and we have suffered because of it. It didn't have to be that way, however. There were always better alternatives each president could have chosen; had they done so, we would be in a stronger, more financially secure place.

Even after the devastating events of September 2001, the U.S. was still in a uniquely powerful military, diplomatic, and economic position. We could have dealt decisively with the attack and yet maintained our position of strength. We could have brought our policies into line with the post-Cold War global realities, which would have maximized our national security, lowered the threats across the board, and increased our economic power. All that was possible – and all that has been squandered.

Today, there can be little debate that our condition internationally is manifestly weaker than it was in 2001. Some of that is due to the recovery and technological advancement of Russia and China. But far too many of our troubles were — and remain — self-inflicted.

Our unwillingness to adapt to a changing world and our attempt to keep China and Russia weakened—instead of building constructive relationships with both that could benefit our security and economy—we have tried to cling to the world of 1992. We have tried to use our military power to solve almost every dispute, and we have resolutely refused to engage diplomatically with other powers (friends and adversaries alike) that could have resulted in beneficial outcomes.

Fortunately, it is not too late to get this right. North Korea still has not launched any nuclear missiles. We have not come to military blows with China. Russia has not gone beyond its thinly disguised support in eastern Ukraine and the Crimea. Our counter-terror capabilities have successfully prevented any major strikes against our homeland since 2001. And we still have not given in to the siren song of choosing a war with Iran. None of the damage caused by our post-Cold War foreign policies is irreversible.

What we desperately need to do is conduct a major reevaluation of the way we interact with the rest of the world. We need to thoroughly analyze the world as it is, not as we fancy it to be, and not through the lens of an "us versus them," zero-sum ideology in which we imagine there are wholly evil regimes or wholly good regimes. That's what this book is intended to help facilitate.

To help set the stage for the changes I will propose in the latter sections of this book, I will first detail my personal experience through four combat deployments and my assignment with what was the Army's signature modernization plan of the early 2000s, the Future Combat Systems.

Through these chapters, the reader will begin to graphically understand why the U.S. won decisively in Desert Storm yet has failed to win any wars since. It will become clear why the wars in Syria, Iraq, Afghanistan, and throughout Africa *can't* be won and should be wound down as soon as possible. And it will become clear also why there is a better way to do foreign policy and how we might—even now, after so many missteps— significantly improve our national security and strengthen our ability to prosper economically.

About the Author

Daniel L. Davis retired from the U.S. Army as a lieutenant colonel after 21 years of active service and currently serves as Senior Fellow and Military Expert for Defense Priorities. He was deployed into combat zones four times: Operation Desert Storm in 1991; Iraq in 2009; and Afghanistan in 2005 and 2011. He was awarded the Bronze Star Medal for Valor at the Battle of 73 Easting in 1991 and awarded a Bronze Star Medal for service in Afghanistan in 2011.

Davis gained national attention in 2012 when he returned from Afghanistan and published a report detailing how senior U.S. military and civilian leaders told the American public and Congress the war was going well while in reality it was headed to defeat. Events since then have confirmed his analysis was correct.

Today he regularly publishes foreign policy and military-related analysis in the nation's premier print outlets and routinely provides expert analysis on national and international television networks. His works have been featured in The New York Times, USA Today, Newsweek, CNN, Fox News, The Guardian (UK), US News & World Report, TIME, Politico, Washington Times, The Hill, and other publications. Davis was also the recipient of the 2012 Ridenhour Prize for Truth-telling. He is a regular guest on Fox News, Fox Business News, BBC, CNN, NewsMax, and other television networks.

He is called to Capitol Hill to provide authoritative testimony at Congressional hearings and conferences, and often as a speaker for foreign policy functions. He lives in the Washington, DC area with his family.

Acknowledgments

I will be forever grateful for the strong support **Rep. Walter Jones** of North Carolina gave me in 2012. After I went public in revealing the truth of the Afghan war, no one backed me more strongly. He had been one of the earliest and most vocal Congressional defenders of the 2003 Iraq war, but after he discovered the intelligence used to justify it had been fraudulent, he turned decisively against pointless wars. He died in office in 2019, and the U.S. lost a great voice of integrity and honor.

Matthew Hoh showed incredible courage in 2009 by resigning from a high-level post in the State Department in protest of Afghan war policies that could only fail. He sacrificed his career to expose the truth in the hope of ending the war and preventing the unnecessary deaths of more American service members and Afghan civilians. His courage inspired me to go forward in 2012, and he has been a dear friend ever since.

Danielle Brian, director of the program on government oversight, had long been a champion and defender of whistleblowers. In late 2011, when she heard about my case, became perhaps my most stalwart supporter. Without her help, encouragement, and friendship, I may never have been able to tell America the truth.

The last time I saw Rep. Jones, in his office in June 2017

Chapter 1: *Setting the Stage*

At a White House speech in May 2019, President Trump made a familiar claim for an American politician: "We have the greatest military, right now, that the world has ever known." As virtually all of the bi-partisan foreign policy establishment for the past 20 years has proven, this belief that we have a near-invincible military has underwritten volumes of bad policy.

Because too many so-called Washington experts believe our armed forces can't be defeated, they show little restraint in using or threatening to use military force abroad. While it is largely true that we have the best-trained and most technologically advanced military, there is a profoundly important caveat that needs to be understood: having a "the greatest" military is not synonymous with "can never be defeated." The unwillingness (or inability) of leading voices to recognize the distinction could one day have catastrophic results for the security of our country.

Given the current composition, organization, and capabilities of the world's top militaries, there is presently no nation on earth that could successfully launch a surprise, unprovoked attack against the U.S. and defeat us. Our strategic and operational ability to absorb any strike and deliver a crushing retaliation is unmatched.

China, Russia, North Korea, and to a lesser extent Iran have the ability on paper to launch conventional attacks against America or our military forces abroad that could be severe and painful. But our 24/7/365 ability to respond is such that the aggressor nation would receive a punishing retaliatory strike literally within minutes. This produces a powerful deterrence to any would-be aggressor.

In the nuclear realm, Russia is the only nation on earth with the ability to wipe out our country. If Moscow did launch an unprovoked nuclear attack, however, they would also be wiped out – and are thus prevented by sheer self-preservation from making such an imprudent, unprovoked attack.

A few others could inflict a bitter blow against us, but we could annihilate any foe who was foolish enough to try—China included—with a lethality they cannot match. That knowledge makes our nuclear deterrence, like our conventional deterrence, uniquely formidable.

However, that is not to suggest American military dominance is absolute. It is not.

As has been amply demonstrated in every war since the end of World War II—Korea, Vietnam, Iraq, Afghanistan, Syria, Yemen, Somalia, Pakistan, *ad infinitum*—even tremendous military power does not automatically translate into political victories.

Blindly sending our military into engagements where it should never be sent—choosing wars against China or Iran, for example—and we may one day suffer a gouging defeat we should never have suffered. Several key areas in our international portfolio urgently need changing, but our relations with Russia and China are the two most pressing.

Before we stumble into any pointless and unnecessary conflicts with either, we must reform the way we conduct foreign policy and bring it into line with current global realities. Doing so will preserve our ability to strike a powerful blow against any attacker while avoiding unnecessary conflicts.

Europe

The first step to modernizing our foreign policy is the recognition that today's global environment is no longer like the one that existed during the heat of the Cold War when most of our current security relationships were formed. NATO was created in 1949 under the still-smoldering wreckage of World War II and as the massive Soviet menace was just beginning to rise. Western Germany was shorn of its eastern half and most of its industry lie in ruins. France and England had suffered grievously, losing more than a million of its citizens to the conflict.

The U.S., however, was the undisputed Western power in both military and economic might. We initially had a nuclear monopoly and an industrial machine undamaged by the war. Through the economic package of the Marshall Plan (which provided billions for European countries to rebuild) and the military pact of NATO, the U.S. was the Western world's indispensable nation.

It is no exaggeration to say that without Uncle Sam's direct and extensive involvement, Europe may have collapsed or succumbed to the infection of communism spreading in the post-war world. Throughout the Cold War, Europe desperately needed American help.

Lord Hastings Ismay, NATO's first secretary general, <u>famously said</u> that NATO existed to "keep the Soviets out, the Americans in, and the Germans down." But with the death of the USSR and the reunification of Germany in the early 1990s—along with the rise of Germany, France, and the UK as rich nations—the fundamental reasons for NATO's existence vanished. The once-compelling justification for the U.S. to underwrite the security of Western Europe also disappeared.

In the 1950s, the main security concerns for the United States were our allies in Western Europe. The Soviet Union and Warsaw Pact alliance would eventually boast 50,000 tanks, thousands of warplanes, and thousands of tactical and strategic nuclear weapons—most of which threatened us and our allies.

Russia, which survived as a rump state following the 1991 disillusion of the Soviet Union, still has the world's largest nuclear weapons inventory and remains the only foe on earth that can destroy the United States. But its conventional power is less than a shadow of its Red Army past, while our nuclear arsenal could wipe out Russia many times over. In fact, many of the countries that once composed a majority of the Warsaw Pact are now NATO members.

What the U.S. desperately needs today is to conduct an honest, updated assessment of the world as it is. We should identify the strengths and weaknesses of our friends and potential adversaries, determine the direction of emerging trends and opportunities, and then establish new policies commensurate with these observed realities and our national interests.

A new, forward-thinking policy won't be to merely ask NATO members in Europe to pay more for having American troops on their soil but to begin methodically and professionally transitioning European security to the Europeans themselves. EU countries, many of whom spend as little as 1 percent of their GDP on their national defense, have not taken responsibility for their security for three main reasons:

First, they believe the U.S. will continue being the first-responders for any threat to their security. Second, they would rather spend their money on their domestic population and let the U.S. pay to keep them safe. Third, as proven by how little they spend on defense, the truth is they regard the threat from Russia to be marginal and manageable (with the pointed exception of the NATO members who live nearest to Russia).

Europe already has a substantial cumulative military advantage over the Russian army in every category and could defeat Russian conventional forces even without U.S. intervention. These nations have the modern economies to fund national militaries that can provide a bigger portion of their defense.

It may not be time to completely mothball the transatlantic alliance yet, but it is most definitely time to transition NATO so that European states take the lead on their security and America shifts to become the strategic reserve. Risking a conventional war with Russia that otherwise poses no direct threat to our country is not a wise policy. Unfortunately, antagonizing the Russian bear isn't the only adversary with whom we risk unnecessary conflict.

Asia-Pacific

Even amid the gash to our economy from coronavirus, there has been considerable discussion suggesting the U.S. should fund new initiatives in the Indo-Pacific to "send a powerful strategic message of U.S. commitment to the region." A careful examination of the fundamentals involved, however, quickly shows that such a plan would deepen the dependencies on the U.S. military by many Asian nations while adding nothing to our security.

Let's cut the crap and call this what it is. This proposed U.S. military buildup in the Asia-Pacific is not about defending "the region." This is about preparing for conflict with China, as Defense Secretary Mark Esper implied, <u>darkly warning</u> that the U.S. would not "cede an inch" to China in that part of the world.

The most critical question that needs to be answered about the utility or necessity of America embarking on such a military-first plan of action: is there evidence that China has both the intent and the capacity (either in the near or medium-term) to *attack* the U.S. or our armed forces? The answer is a resounding 'no.'

To be sure, as senior Pentagon leaders have <u>correctly pointed out</u>, China has made substantial improvements in its military. What we must ascertain, however, is the extent to which these military improvements portend a threat to American security. Such analysis quickly reveals that China's military buildup is designed to *defend* its territory against the U.S., not *invade* other nations (except Taiwan; more on that below).

China's decades-long military buildup has served to modernize its forces and harden its defenses against American attack; in military-speak, it's A2/AD, Anti Access/Area Denial, to Chinese territory.

This system develops, employs, and synchronizes technology, drones, missiles, command-and-control assets, warships, anti-air assets, and space forces into an integrated ability to repel a theoretical U.S. force as far away from Chinese territory as possible. A2/AD is unquestionably a potent and effective deterrent to external attack. It's what is missing from this buildup, however, that is most instructive for *American* security.

For all China's development of the past 30 years, it still lacks the equipment and technology necessary to guarantee success in conducting the relatively short and easy cross-strait invasion of what Beijing considers the breakaway province of Taiwan.

Since the Chinese Communist Party (CCP) troops defeated the Chinese Nationalists in their 1949 civil war, the CCP has constantly and unambiguously stated they would use force to reunify Taiwan should the island declare independence. Yet in the 70 years since the end of their civil war, China still has insufficient military infrastructure to guarantee a successful invasion and capture of Taiwan. A 2019 Pentagon report concludes, for example, that any attempt, "to invade Taiwan would likely strain China's armed forces and invite international intervention."

If it would strain China to the breaking point just to invade this one small island, there is no rational case to be made that China has any significant territorial ambitions beyond its borders. Decades of development of its A2/AD capabilities show that defense of its territory – not foreign conquest—is what China values and where the bulk of its investments lie. Furthermore, America's unrivaled ability to project power around the world makes it a physical impossibility for China to attack any American territory.

There is no utility, therefore, in significantly increasing American military power in the Indo-Pacific region for the primary purpose of "thwarting" an alleged Chinese threat to other nations in the region. In fact, expanding American military power in the Pacific region works against our interests by ensuring other states spend less on their national security because they believe there's a good chance we'll do it for them.

For Asia-Pacific countries concerned of a potential military threat from China, we should be willing to provide them with advanced weaponry to build their own A2/AD defensive system. They can buy this, rather than getting it free from the U.S., to make any attack by China so costly for the attackers that Beijing is deterred from even attempting one.

Each nation in that region should be responsible for funding its defense to the level it deems appropriate to the threat. The defense of other wealthy Asian nations should not, under any circumstances, be the primary responsibility of the American taxpayer. The U.S. military should defend *our* country and ensure the prosperity–first and foremost–of *our* citizens. That's not to suggest we should withdraw from international affairs, however. Far from it.

Other Regions of the Globe – and a Change of Thinking

The United States should *expand* our engagement with the rest of the world, not shrink from it. Our security and ability to prosper will never be as strong as they could be if we were to withdraw from the world and form our own little "Fortress America." However—and this is a big "however"—we have for too long measured our level of "global leadership" in direct proportion to the number of combat troops we have deployed abroad. That is a profoundly bad correlation to make.

As I will discuss in the following chapters, by predicating our foreign policy on having and regularly using lethal military force abroad, we not only weaken our national security, but we poison our relations with friend and foe alike. We limit our ability to advance economic opportunities for our population and tarnish our ability to effectively influence others in ways beneficial to our interests and values.

Instead of making all our international engagement military-based, we need to increase and deepen our diplomatic engagement. We need to emphasize solutions to common problems that feature more engagement with our friends and allies, actively listening to them more, and including them in the deliberation process. Doing so will gain us access to more opportunities for our people and we will benefit from the thoughts and ideas of other smart people.

Engagement would also extend to competitors and, to some level, even our adversaries. Conventional wisdom today rejects that idea, holding that we don't talk to those whose actions we don't like. Often the bad behavior we identify is indeed reprehensible. But this conventional thinking ignores what ought to be an obvious truth: if you're not talking to those with whom you disagree, if you're not engaged with the leaders of countries whose behavior you dislike, it is impossible to have even the chance of mitigating or changing said behavior.

We've got to acknowledge the simple human reality that no one—and no country—is all good or all bad. The best of our allies have aspects that we find disagreeable or problematic, and even the worst of our adversaries have some redeeming qualities. To pretend that our friends are entirely good means we'll fail to acknowledge or address areas where they fall short; pretending our adversaries are all bad means we'll fail to acknowledge and affirm behaviors that we find positive.

When we demonize opponents and glorify friends we limit our ability to influence either. That's to our detriment. It is time we replace a foreign policy that traffics too much in the realm of wishful thinking and adopt a more mature and intelligent way of engaging with the world.

I will begin to lay out that vision in the following chapters. First, I'll examine Operation Desert Storm in 1991 and my participation in the Battle of 73 Easting. That will provide the foundation for examining what went into developing the devastatingly capable American armed forces that existed on the eve of Desert Storm.

From there, the scene transitions to my assignment with what was then the Army's premier modernization program, the Future Combat Systems (FCS), at Fort Bliss, Texas in 2007. The FCS was billed as a futuristic modernization program that would catapult the U.S. into a dominant global position for decades to come. Unfortunately, based on my experience during Desert Storm, I quickly realized that the program was terribly flawed. Had we continued down that path beyond 2007, I've argued, we would be in grave danger of stumbling into a future in which we might unnecessarily lose a fight we should otherwise have won easily.

Next, we'll examine the war in Afghanistan and look at the reasons we got involved in the first place. Then I will detail the shifting objectives and strategies that two administrations adopted that set the stage for sinking us into a permanent, unwinnable war. This chapter will conclude by looking at the run-up to Obama's unnecessary surge in 2009 and ending by examining my second deployment to that war in 2010-11. This chapter will expose in painful detail why the war will never be won and why we will fight there forever if we don't end it on our terms and withdraw.

Right on the heels of that chapter, I'll look forward, examining and presenting ways that can end our foreign policy losing streak and start to rebuild a more effective and productive policy. I first devote an entire chapter to solving the most pressing and vexing problem we face: ending the forever-wars.

A good bit of the fear Americans have in supporting an end to our various wars is the belief that to do so would make us unnecessarily vulnerable to a new 9/11-style attack. That is an unfounded fear. After exposing the logical and rational reasons why we should not be afraid of that, I present an effective way to end the wars that will end the destructive waste of blood and treasure, and actually *increase* our overall national security.

In the final chapter, I outline the basis for a comprehensive reform of how we conduct foreign policy. An entire book would be necessary to detail the things we'd need to change in each region of the world, but this chapter provides the general intellectual foundation from which a new policy would be built. The chapter surveys how our relations would need to change. primarily in Russia, China, Iran, North Korea, the Middle East in general.

American foreign policy barely changed after the end of the Cold War and has almost stood still since the horrific events of 9/11 – and we have suffered because of it. Though the damage done so far has been real, it is not too late to turn things around. The people in this country have historically shown themselves to be creative, resilient, and forward-thinking. I'm counting on that characteristic to emerge again.

Chapter 2: *The Battle of 73 Easting Against the Iraqi Republican Guard*

Then-Captain H.R. McMaster and Davis, posing with McMaster's tank following Battle of 73 Easting, March 1991.

Knowledge of Desert Storm these days is frequently limited to the basics: the United States deployed a massive land army to eject Saddam Hussein from Kuwait in 1991 following his illegal invasion the year before. We then withdrew. As a green 2nd lieutenant who happened to have been placed at the center of the most fierce and violent tank battle of that war, however, I have a different—and vivid—recollection.

Except for one fateful, seemingly minor decision I made less than a year before Saddam's invasion, I would never have been in the fight at all. To explain why that decision was made, let me rewind a few years.

When I was in college in the early 1980s I had some skills as a point guard in basketball. I had a furious desire (my parents considered it an obsession!) to make the basketball team at Texas Tech University in Lubbock as a walk-on. The coach in the 1980s was a tough disciplinarian named <u>Gerald Myers</u>, who, for reasons I have never understood, allowed me to walk on to his program in the fall of 1984 with no high school experience. Perhaps he saw that I had some base level of talent, or perhaps he was intrigued by the driving passion to succeed he saw in me.

I wished God had allowed me to develop basketball skills earlier in my life so I could have gotten a solid year or two of playing experience in high school. But you can't change what never happened, and despite the absence of that opportunity, I had a chance to play for a major college team. I was going to be relentless in my determination and preparation.

I didn't care if my chances were low; I didn't care that all the other players had impressive high school pedigrees. I intended to beat all the other walk-ons to earn a roster spot. If I could get on the team, I believed, I could then gain enough experience to become something special.

Ultimately, I didn't want to just *be* on the team. My goals were higher: I wanted to be an integral part of helping Texas Tech win a championship. I had the audacity to dream that one day, if everything went my way and I met my goals at Tech, I could play in the NBA. As a Texas native who had lived most of his life in the Dallas-Fort Worth area, I dreamt of draining three-pointers for the Dallas Mavericks.

After a couple of months of intense training and conditioning in late 1984, it was nearly time for Myers to make his final selections and set the roster for the season. Beyond the scholarship slots that had already been set, he had one final slot to assign. There were only two walk-ons left at that point, me and one other fellow. I was a 6-foot point guard and he was a 6-foot-5-inch forward. As it turned out, Myers needed forward help on the team more than another guard. I wasn't picked.

Though I knew going in my chances were small, I nevertheless actually expected to make the team. I went into a mini-depression in the immediate aftermath of my failure. It was very hard to attend games that season, seeing my friends playing while I watched helplessly from the stands, my passion to play undiminished. But life goes on despite the disappointments. It was time to move on.

Next year, for several personal and financial reasons, I decided to take a break from my college career and join the U.S. Army as a private. I would serve for two years, mostly in Germany, in a Multiple-Launch Rocket System battalion in a tiny village called Babenhausen (now only a husk of an abandoned, <u>ghost town</u> in Germany).

I arrived in Babenhausen in 1986, still in the heat of the Cold War. Ronald Reagan's famous "<u>Tear down this wall</u>" speech was still a year away. At the time, though, I have to admit I was loving serving in the MLRS battalion, going to live-fire drills where we regularly fired our rockets and — most of all — spent a lot of time in our combat vehicles driving through the rolling hills and small villages of the German countryside. Honestly, much of this was fun.

Though things would change when I would return to Germany as an officer several years later, at the time I gave very little consideration to the possibility that our frequent field exercises could one day become real combat against Soviet troops. What did occur to me, however, was that while I enjoyed aspects of Army life, a career as an enlisted man was not in the cards for me. If I was going to continue serving, I believed my skills and temperament were better suited to being an officer.

Davis playing with the Army team from Fort Sill, OK against Texas Tech in Lubbock, TX, November 1989

While in Babenhausen, I was able to satiate part of my desire when I earned a spot on a German club basketball team near my Army base not far from Darmstadt. In 1987, I returned to Texas Tech to finish my degree and get my commission as an Army officer, so I spent two years in the ROTC program. After graduation in 1989, I was commissioned as a second lieutenant and assigned to the field artillery branch.

I was sent to Fort Sill, Oklahoma, to attend the artillery school for junior officers to learn the basics of the trade before going on to a regular Army assignment. Near the end of the course and just before graduation, I was given the chance to attend airborne training at Fort Benning, Georgia. As an avid student of military history, I have always been fascinated with the heroic exploits of the 101st and 82nd Airborne Divisions, especially their actions in Normandy in 1944 in support of the D-Day landings. The chance to finally get my airborne wings was incredibly appealing and something I would have loved to do.

However…

During my time at Fort Sill, I had continued my love of playing basketball on the Army team, which traveled the region playing other Army and Air Force base teams. As it turned out, Fort Sill was planning on playing *against Texas Tech* in an exhibition game in Lubbock before the start of the 1989 regular season.

America was still fully engaged in the Cold War. The Soviet Union had existed for more than 70 years at that time, and, as far as any of us knew, they'd be there another 70. So, I figured I'd have plenty of opportunities to take airborne training, but this would be a once-in-a-lifetime chance to fulfill, at least in a small way, my earlier dream to play at Tech.

I decided against airborne school, which would have started in late 1989 or early 1990, so I could play in that game, an experience I never forgot. Because I declined the airborne school, I was given a regular duty assignment when I graduated in November 1989. When I got my notification, it said, "2nd Squadron, 2nd Armored Cavalry Regiment (2/2 ACR) in Bamberg, Germany."

In November 1989, going to war in the Middle East was not even considered a distant possibility. I was more excited about returning to Germany and possibly playing more basketball than joining an armored cavalry regiment.

In fact, I had no idea what "the Cav" (as an armored cavalry regiment is often called) was, but my classmates at the artillery school who did said it was an awesome opportunity. I previously served only in artillery units and thus had little knowledge of armored units. But I was eager to learn.

Initially, I was assigned to the squadron howitzer battery, which consists of eight 155mm cannons, as a fire support officer for Eagle Troop in Second Squadron. That meant I would perform duty as the troop maneuver commander's primary advisor to help him incorporate cannon and rocket fire into his battle plan. I would then coordinate with higher headquarters in the artillery units to attack targets during the fight while the commander focused on the direct fire engagements with enemy armor and infantry.

My commander of Eagle Troop was an officer nearing the end of his career. He was, to be charitable, poorly skilled at leading men and not very nimble in his thinking. He was a nice man, but that's not a good attribute for a commander with so much firepower at his disposal.

An armored cavalry troop was then composed of about 120 men, nine M1A1 Abrams main battle tanks, 12 M2 Cavalry Fighting Vehicles, and two M106 4.2" mortar carriers. I accompanied the battle group in my armored fire support vehicle equipped with long-range optics and numerous radio networks, manned by myself and two crewmen.

But that version of Eagle Troop did not function as a team. Because the commander was weak, some of the stronger personalities in the unit, other lieutenants and some sergeants, filled the void and led as best they could, but often in opposition to one another; the rest of us were left to navigate the chaos and try to choose which leaders we would follow. As a result, we did poorly in every graded maneuver exercise and field training during that commander's tenure.

The main mission of 2/2 ACR was to patrol the still-active border between East and West Germany and protect against enemy incursion with live ammunition. On the other side of the border were communist

East German mechanized units and some USSR combat troops. We had known, for decades, that at any time the Soviets could come flooding across the border and attack to the west. Thus, our secondary mission was to prepare to defend Western Europe, and we trained a great deal across sometimes vast tracts of West German countryside.

The training opportunities were excellent, the experience invaluable, but morale in Eagle Troop was near rock bottom because of the leadership void. That changed in March 1990 when Eagle Troop got a new commander, Captain H.R. McMaster. He would later go on as a full colonel to <u>command</u> the 3rd Armored Cavalry Regiment in the troubled early part of Operation Iraqi Freedom in 2005, and ultimately became President Trump's national security advisor as a lieutenant general in <u>February 2017</u>.

McMaster and I became good friends and would remain so for 20 years until we had an unfortunate falling out in 2011 over differences of opinion in Afghanistan. But in the spring of 1990, I was thrilled to be serving under him. He had an electric personality, was incredibly knowledgeable for a young captain, and a strong leader. The culture and environment in Eagle Troop turned around overnight.

With hardly any change in the rest of the troop's personnel, McMaster transformed Eagle into what would eventually become the premier company-level fighting formation in the entire regiment. In May, we deployed to the Combat Maneuver Training Center at Hohenfels, Germany, where we would conduct force-on-force maneuver exercises in which two armored units were outfitted with equipment that would replicate the effects of various weapons on the targets, coming as close as possible to allowing a unit of tanks and armored vehicles to train as they would in a real war.

In one particular mock battle, the squadron commander, who had marginal leadership skills, made several mistakes during the early phases of the battle and tried to correct his deficiencies by giving McMaster (whom he particularly disliked) a near-impossible task: defend against a mechanized battalion, on his own, while the rest of the squadron engaged elsewhere. It was a virtual die-in-place order.

McMaster called the officers into a hasty meeting to discuss the new battle plans. I distinctly remember watching H.R.'s face during the meeting turn increasingly red with anger as he looked intently at the battle map, contemplating the foolishness of the mission he had been given. McMaster saw clearly how his boss had essentially offered up Eagle Troop as a sacrificial lamb while the squadron commander organized the other troops for a defense elsewhere in the sector.

McMaster stared at the map, without speaking, for what seemed like an eternity. For all his excellent qualities, he had an explosive temper that could be quite unpleasant when it was directed at you. We all braced for the explosion. But it never came. Instead, after staring intently at the entire battle area on the map, his face suddenly changed and his mood brightened. He then calmly announced he had formed a plan – which did not include dying in place.

Despite what the squadron commander had anticipated, McMaster had no intention of serving as a speed bump to slow the enemy advance. He devised a plan that would instead deal a lethal blow to the entire enemy battalion. He set off in his typically rapid-fire method telling each of us what we were supposed to do, when, and in what sequence. My jaw dropped. All I could see when my inexperienced lieutenant eyes looked at the map was certain defeat; McMaster had come up with a plan that gave us a chance to surprise the enemy and win.

Me with fellow Eagle Troop lieutenant John Hillen, after a German training exercise pre-Desert Storm.

We junior officers had limited time to go back to our platoons and vehicles to prepare our crews for the mission. It was a race against time to see if we could get ready before the lead enemy tanks came into range. We did as much as we could, and when the word came that enemy tanks were closing in, we stopped and got into position. McMaster then led us in a lightning strike against the unsuspecting enemy — which had outnumbered us nearly three to one — and destroyed the entire battalion in a remarkably synchronized surprise attack that lasted all of 12 minutes. We suffered zero casualties.

That was a training event. But little did any of us know that mere months from that moment, we would execute a very similar scenario halfway across the world in a live combat engagement that would play out in a very similar way and with the same outcome.

I had joined 2/2 ACR without any idea what the cavalry was. My first exposure to cav life was decidedly negative, and I was already regretting returning to the Army, anxious to complete my three-year service obligation so I could get out and start work in the civilian world, where I wanted to coach high school football and basketball. But when McMaster entered the scene and showed me what true leadership could do, that all changed. Radically.

I had been a part of a remarkable success in that training engagement. In the process, I came to understand more about the cavalry mindset, became good friends with my fellow armor lieutenants in Eagle Troop, and discovered that I was pretty good at my job. I think anytime you're good at something you naturally start to like it more, and that's exactly how it worked for me.

Another key reason I began to develop a real pride in being a cavalry officer was the arrival of the new squadron operations officer, then Major Douglas Macgregor. He had joined the squadron about the same time as McMaster and likewise represented a dramatic improvement in the quality of leadership in the headquarters.

Macgregor would later be promoted to lieutenant colonel and command a cavalry squadron that would be uniquely successful in peacetime training, literally <u>writing the book(s)</u> on how to modernize and reform the Department of Defense. As of this writing, he <u>was nominated</u> by President Trump to be the ambassador to Germany.

It was immediately clear to me in 1990 that even though Macgregor had the modest rank of major, he was intellectually and emotionally light years ahead of his peers. The thing that distinguished Macgregor, however, wasn't merely his above-average knowledge and ability to train the squadron for war, it was his unusual self-confidence.

He was not arrogant in the sense of some men who believe themselves to be the smartest and the best, but in a deeper, more meaningful way. He was never threatened by people who showed themselves to be smart or capable in any given area. He did not, as even some highly accomplished leaders can, seek to diminish those around him so that he could appear even bigger.

When we met, I was barely six months into my first assignment as a lieutenant with very little experience and limited knowledge of warfighting. By all rights, I should only have been allowed to listen to and learn from Macgregor from a distance. But several times he sought my input and asked me questions about various aspects of training and providing fire support. He offered me a chance to weigh in on combat matters when we went to war. It always amazed me that he cared what I, a nobody-lieutenant, thought. It wasn't just me, though; Macgregor treated nearly everyone like that.

What he *didn't* do well in those early years, however, was show patience with arrogant or presumptuous officers who thought more of themselves than their performance merited. He was especially dismissive of those with high rank and limited ability. He got into trouble on more than one occasion for giving voice to his low opinion of someone who outranked him.

I wished he'd kept his tongue on a tighter leash in those early years (in which case he would have had fewer roadblocks to his career), but I won't lie: his willingness to listen to subordinates and show the courage to sometimes excoriate those who outranked him raised his stature immensely in our eyes. Nearly all of us were willing to do anything he asked when it came to the life-and-death business of armored combat. Our confidence in him would be justified when the bullets started flying for real the following year.

The countdown to war for 2/2 ACR began while we were engaged in a training exercise in late July 1990. The exercises took place at the

Grafenwoehr training center in Germany, where we were scheduled to take part in one of the exercises I liked most. At "Graf," as soldiers commonly refer to it, a military organization would conduct individual and platoon-level training in an expansive maneuver area fenced off from German civil society.

After a few days of that, we moved to troop-level training, culminating in a large-scale exercise in which the entire cavalry squadron conducted war games on the Graf installation. Upon completion, we then shifted to a live-fire range where we shot 155mm cannons, machine guns, and tank main gun rounds at mock enemy targets, before finally leaving Graf to conduct maneuvers over large sections of the German countryside. The intent was to replicate in real time on the ground what we expected would happen if the Red Army invaded west.

The Warsaw Pact nations east of West Germany, anchored by the Soviet Union, had more than 50,000 tanks and millions of troops in 1990. Because of the terrain in Central Europe, there was always the risk that communist forces could come flooding across a large plain known as the Fulda Gap and defeat the nations of Western Europe. The 2/2 ACR was one of several units charged with defending the East/West border.

On Aug. 2, 1990, Eagle Troop along with the rest of the 2nd Squadron was at Grafenwoehr preparing to maneuver our nine tanks and 12 Bradleys throughout the German countryside, engaging in a mock battle. Before we left our assembly areas for the operation, however, something distracted us from halfway across the world.

Saddam Hussein, the dictator of Iraq, had done what we feared the Soviets might: He sent hundreds of tanks and other armored vehicles <u>flooding across their southern border</u> to Kuwait in an unexpected attack and quickly subdued the Kuwait military. At the end of the operation, Iraqi tanks were a mere three miles from the Saudi border, representing a dagger at the throat of the oil supply on which most of the Western world depended.

Before we had even left our assembly areas the next day, McMaster and Macgregor adjusted our training to reflect the possibility that we, as a cavalry organization tasked with making first contact against enemy armored formations, would be called upon to fight Saddam's troops. Since our terrific performance at the training center the previous May, McMaster and I had developed an excellent working relationship and began collaborating on his battle plans.

On Aug. 5, as we prepared to launch a troop-level exercise at Graf ahead of the squadron-level training that would come later, McMaster and I had the strange feeling that the crisis in Kuwait would eventually draw us into a war. It didn't make a lot of sense at that time—the 2nd ACR had not been deployed in combat since World War II. It was the 11th ACR (another cavalry unit performing border duty) that won battle glory in Vietnam, and, if anyone from Germany went to Kuwait, most believed it would be the 11th, not us.

Nevertheless, something seemed to simultaneously convince us both that 2/2 ACR would fight in the Middle East. Before beginning the exercise, McMaster solemnly addressed a gathering of the troop leaders outside the troops' barracks: "Men, we must take very seriously what we are about to do," he began. "It is possible that the next operations order I give will be in the sands of Iraq." There was an eerie sense of unease because, as he spoke, a gust of wind ominously stirred up a big dust cloud that settled over the gathering.

At that point, we realized that what had just a few days ago seemed like another routine military exercise was now shaping up to be a final preparation for combat operations. We completed that three-week exercise with a renewed sense of focus.

After we returned to our home base at Bamberg, Germany, the standoff on the Saudi-Kuwaiti border continued to sizzle. President Bush had quickly deployed the 101st and 82nd Airborne Divisions to Saudi Arabia to act as a deterrent to further Iraqi aggression. While excellent and well-trained, those were light infantry divisions that would be at a severe disadvantage should the armored and mechanized Iraqi divisions choose to attack.

It wasn't hard to figure out that if the president thought there was any chance of actual combat operations, he would need to deploy heavy armor as well. If the Pentagon selected 2nd ACR to serve as an armored vanguard in such a fight, the squadron's leadership began to shift the focus of our training and professional development from one that was Europe-centric to how large mechanized formations would conduct operations in open deserts.

In September 1990, Macgregor, *expecting* that at some point we would be alerted for deployment, began teaching the squadron's officers and senior enlisted troops about World War II tank battles in the North African desert. One of his favorite topics was the battle between Rommel's Panzerarmee Afrika and the British Eighth Army.

Macgregor spent the majority of his time training us on the pivotal Gazala Battles and the June 1942 fall of the British-held fortress at Tobruk in North Africa. In these battles, Rommel's forces were sometimes outnumbered three-to-one by the British. Macgregor pointed out that numbers alone do not determine the outcome of battles, but leadership, sound strategy, and violently executed plans will usually win the day. That training represented only a hypothetical possibility at that moment.

That potential turned into cold reality, however, when on Nov. 8, 1990, Secretary of Defense <u>Dick Cheney announced</u> from the White House that the 2nd Armored Cavalry Regiment would be among the heavy forces from Europe that would deploy to the Middle East in a major buildup of combat power.

The next day, we began preparing our tanks and other combat vehicles for deployment aboard fast transport ships for the trip from the German port of Bremerhaven to the Saudi Arabian port of Al Jubayl. During the weeks it would take the ships to arrive at the Saudi port, Macgregor super-charged the professional development program to deepen our understanding of armored tactics in the desert.

Less than a month after Cheney's order, the troops boarded planes and touched down into the heat of a Saudi desert. Immediately upon arrival we began painting our vehicles desert tan and loading them with live ammunition. We did everything with an earnestness, eager to deploy just south of the Saudi border with Kuwait in anticipation of the order to attack, which we all assumed would come quickly.

The role of the cavalry in modern warfare is similar to what it has been throughout antiquity: to be the first into the battle zone conducting reconnaissance to discover the location, strength, and intention of the enemy, trying to clear up uncertainty and turn chaos into an advantage for our side. Once the cavalry determines the true picture of the enemy, our mission would be to engage them, fix them in place, and open a path for the heavily armored divisions following behind us that would complete the enemy's destruction.

The cavalry's role appealed to me greatly. I *love* operating in chaos, in environments of uncertainty, when there is no road map or instruction booklet to chart the way. We learn the fundamentals of combat and then memorize and endlessly rehearse battle drills so that when we make unexpected contact with the enemy we instantly and violently react, neutralizing the threat.

While uncertainty makes many people uncomfortable, others relish being risk-takers and enjoy trying to make sense of chaos. Both Macgregor and McMaster were experts in this area. It seemed neither was ever caught unaware, never taken by surprise. No matter what happened, no matter how quickly things may have unfolded, they always reassessed the situation and developed a new plan on the fly. So far as I was able to observe during all the exercises and combat operations I took part in under these two leaders, I never saw them fail to dominate the unexpected.

One dramatic example happened even before we engaged our first Iraqi soldier. As soon as the vehicles were unloaded and prepared for combat operations at Jubyl, the regiment headed for the Kuwaiti border to begin final training before attack day, known as "G-Day." In an amazing series of events during one such exercise, McMaster came within a hair's breadth of suffering an accident that almost caused him to miss the attack altogether.

Because we had trained most of our careers in the forests and rolling hills of Europe, we had to rapidly adjust our techniques for the desert.

Shortly after arriving in the border region, Macgregor directed the squadron to conduct a simulated and complex night assault. The desert on a moonless night is so dark you quite literally cannot see your hand in front of your face. (I know. I actually tried to see my hand!) Using early generations of night vision goggles, we began the challenge of navigating in the dark when we could see no terrain and could only barely make out our own vehicles.

As McMaster's fire support officer, I was in my armored fire support vehicle following about 100 meters directly behind his tank as he maneuvered across the desert. At a certain point, he began giving radio instructions for the troop to change the plan and move toward a new objective.

From my position behind McMaster, I looked through my night vision goggles and suddenly saw the silhouettes of two Bradleys driving directly into his path from his left. I reached for the radio to warn him of the approaching danger, but he was still in the process of giving orders over his radio. Unlike with a phone where a person can both talk and hear at the same time, once a person presses the talk button on the handset of a military radio, they can't hear any other voices. I was unable to break in and helplessly watched in horror as the armored vehicles moved directly into McMaster's path.

My hope that the Bradley driver or commander might see the tank and turn away at the last second were dashed when I saw a hail of sparks fly when the gun tube on McMaster's tank speared directly into the side of the lead Bradley, causing both vehicles to lurch to one side and come to an immediate stop.

My first thought was, "Oh my God. We've killed American soldiers!" The gun tube had penetrated the crew compartment of the Bradley, and I could not imagine how that could happen without killing someone in the cabin—or worse, from my perspective, that the jolt had seriously wounded McMaster or his crew. I raced to the scene and discovered that, miraculously, no one in either vehicle had suffered so much as a scratch.

We later discovered that in the confusion of the squadron's first large-scale night maneuver, two vehicles from a sister troop had lost their way, separated from their unit, and stumbled into McMaster's path trying to find their headquarters. It is sobering to consider that if that gun tube had hit just a fraction of a second later, it would have killed some of the troops and likely ended McMaster's career before the first shot was fired—or that the impact could have caused his tank ammunition to explode, possibly killing everyone in both vehicles.

As I stood near the base of his tank and assessed the damage to both vehicles, I expected we would wait until an armored tow truck arrived to take his vehicle to the squadron maintenance bay. Instead, as soon as McMaster had determined that no one had been seriously wounded in either vehicle and that his tank was still operable, he continued the mission without pause.

I knew McMaster was mission-focused, but I figured—incorrectly, as it turned out—that he would make allowances for a training accident. In his mind, he wasn't on an exercise but simulating a combat mission. If the operation had been in enemy territory, he wouldn't have considered stopping for a mere mishap, so he didn't stop the exercise, either.

As it turned out, the jolt had knocked his gun tube out of alignment, so it would have to be repaired before he could fire his 120mm main gun again. But it didn't prevent him from continuing to command-and-control the troop from his vehicle. When the other Eagle Troopers and I saw the commander making no provisions for failure, not stopping even for a serious accident, we became more determined to do whatever was necessary, no matter what might happen once we crossed the line of departure into enemy territory.

I took this picture during a training exercise in the Saudi desert prior to the attack

With each exercise, the troopers of 2/2 ACR grew in confidence. Some experts predicted the U.S. would win the war because of our superior technology and quality soldiers, but they still suggested Iraq's "elite Republican Guards Corps" – as the media often referred to them as – would fight fanatically. Military planners expected lead U.S. cavalry units could suffer up to 10 percent casualties in the first battles.

More than once, I remember looking around at my fellow Eagle Troopers and wondering which 10 or 12 might never come home—or if *I* would ever come home. Despite this sobering expectation, there was no fear among the troops. Macgregor had so thoroughly prepared the squadron physically and mentally for combat that when the time to attack came, we were not merely willing to engage enemy armor, we *thirsted* for it.

After weeks of air and missile attacks, G-Day was set to be February 23, 1991. Before moving out of our assembly areas for the assault, Macgregor went to visit every unit to give them final instructions in person. He felt the men should see their leaders eye to eye before battle. When he arrived at Eagle Troop headquarters, McMaster assembled all the unit's lieutenants and sergeants to meet him. Macgregor had a reputation for being an inspirational speaker, and we were eager to hear what he had to say.

He started by setting up a battle map, going over the squadron plans, and reiterating Eagle Troop's role in it. Next, he reminded us that we would succeed because we had superior equipment, we were well trained at both the individual and unit level, and, he emphasized, because we were elite cavalrymen. We were the ones the V Corps commander was going to send into battle first to set the stage for overall success.

Finally, he said, there was one overriding factor that would mark the difference between success and failure on the battlefield. "Leadership," he said. "Rommel, who was the commander of the entire German Army in Africa, led from the front. Gentlemen, our men deserve nothing less. There is no substitute for leading this way. I will be up front and I expect you to be there as well." Just days later we would see first-hand the chaos and unpredictability of war and would witness Macgregor and McMaster both living out their every word: from the front, under enemy fire, and clearly in charge.

The day of the attack on enemy territory finally arrived. The squadron was arrayed in battle formation, starting with Fox Troop and Hawk Company in the lead, followed by Ghost Troop and Eagle Troop. The plan was for our 155mm artillery battalion and supporting MLRS rocket battalions to fire a heavy artillery barrage on what we suspected were Iraqi defensive positions right across the Kuwaiti border. But the initial attack on Feb. 23 proved to be rather anticlimactic.

Intelligence had told us there would likely be various border outposts ready to attack us as soon as we penetrated their defenses. But after we blew holes through the border barriers and fired hundreds of artillery shells, and once we drove through the breach we discovered only a few confused goats and a handful of empty buildings. We knew the main line of defense was far to the north, but we had honestly hoped to engage enemy troops immediately. We were quite disappointed when none materialized.

One of Eagle Troop's tanks after we crossed the border into Kuwait and began moving north.

As the famous Army dictum says, no plan survives first contact, so we did what cavalrymen are trained to do when things don't work out as planned: We adjusted. We headed north to find the enemy armor that had burrowed itself in the Kuwaiti sands.

Satellite imagery showed various belts of defending Iraqi infantry units that had been callously placed there by ruthless Iraqi leaders to soak up American bullets in the early phases of the war; the enemy leaders were unconcerned that forcing infantry units to directly engage U.S. tanks would likely be condemning thousands of their soldiers to pointless slaughter.

They hoped that by the time we got to Iraq's formidable Republican Guard tank units in the north, we would be weakened and pose less of a threat. As it turned out, however, the Iraqi infantrymen were not as eager to lose their lives as Saddam was to sacrifice them.

As we advanced to about 60 miles from the Republican Guards, we saw small groups of Iraqi soldiers leaving their bunkers or vehicles to surrender. Most offered no resistance, coming out with hands raised. At first, we processed them as prisoners of war and sped them to the rear for interrogation. The farther north we went, however, so many of them rushed out to surrender that we didn't have the resources to process them. Instead, we just waved at them to move south – and they did.

From Feb. 23-25, we saw only sporadic fighting, processed surrendering troops, and mindlessly rolled across endless tracts of empty desert as our eyes grew red from the blazing intensity of the sun. The temperature in the Middle Eastern deserts can climb upwards of 130 degrees in the summer, but we were there in the winter and sometimes the nights were so cold we had frost on our tanks in the morning.

At sunset Feb. 25, we were greeted with something we never expected in the Kuwait desert: a heavy, soaking, and cold rain. As the commander of my armored fire support vehicle, I had to ride with the hatch open. There was nowhere to hide from the driving rain, and I was drenched, cold, and miserable.

By dawn the next morning, the rain had stopped but the clouds remained. Our procedure when attacking was to lead with our helicopter scouts to screen about six miles in front of our lead cavalry scouts. Having the air cav units identifying the location of the enemy troops would ordinarily give us a significant advantage: the ability to develop the situation against our foe before engaging in direct fire-fights. But barely had we started that day when a sandstorm emerged out of nowhere.

It was a storm of biblical proportions, propelled by an intense wind that made the sand sting when it hit any exposed skin. The helicopters were quickly grounded, leaving our advanced scouts as the first line of defense. I was co-located with the lead scout section of Eagle's Red Platoon of Cavalry Fighting Vehicles.

Because of the thickness of the sandstorm, our otherwise superior optics were seriously degraded; we could barely see 100 yards using googles to protect our naked eyes. Some of the greatest advantages we would

Squadron armored vehicles during the march north towards the Republican Guard

ordinarily hold over the enemy had now been neutralized. If we encountered Iraqi tanks before the sandstorm lifted, we would be at a disadvantage because the Iraqi troops would be in dug-in positions while we would be vulnerable in the open.

About 3 p.m., one of the scout leaders from Red Platoon radioed me to say he saw something in his CFV's thermal sights but wasn't sure what it was. My vehicle was less than 100 yards away, so I made the quick drive and jumped into his turret to look through the viewfinder.

As soon as I did, my eyes opened wide, and I shouted that I thought this was the line of dug-in enemy tanks we'd been seeking for the past two days. All we could see were "hot spots" on the reticles of the gun sights – maybe two miles to our front, but we weren't able to identify the shapes as specific vehicles. Based on how they were arrayed to the front, however, I suspected they were tanks dug into the ground so only the turrets were visible.

I ran back to my vehicle to radio the commander to report the sighting and request permission to engage with long-range artillery. This was, I admit excitedly thinking, "My first kill of the day!" I got on the radio connecting me to the artillery battalion fire direction center and excitedly began sending targeting data for the tanks to my front. Because of the severe dust storm, the enemy, who didn't have thermal viewfinders, had no way of seeing us and would be sitting ducks. I was almost giddy with excitement as I started making the call for fire.

Suddenly, from the corner of my eye, I saw a huge fireball and an explosion. "Oh my God," I immediately thought, "the Iraqi tank must have seen us and Red 6 has been hit!" But as I looked up, I realized that the CFV parked next to me—a mere 20 feet from my head—had just launched the first anti-tank missile from his vehicle launcher toward the enemy armor we had spotted.

"No!" I thought, "those are *my* tanks! I get to destroy them first!" But it was too late. I watched the relatively slow flight of the missile and was treated to a rather spectacular view as the warhead scored a direct hit, apparently detonating in the tank's ammunition storage rack, sending a fireball more than 50 feet into the air.

Now aware that there were confirmed Iraqi tanks in our zone of attack, McMaster gave instructions to Eagle Troop to maneuver toward the enemy. Initially, he permitted me to launch an artillery strike as he continued to maneuver forward with Eagle's tanks. But cannons to the rear couldn't process the mission in time and the order had to be scrapped. Our troops were advancing too fast and might fall under our bombs.

Because enemy contact was now likely, McMaster changed the formation. Instead of leading with the lighter-skinned armor of the scouts, he moved the troop's nine tanks to the front. Macgregor had always told us that the safest place to be on the battlefield was in an M1 tank driving directly towards the gun tube of *any* enemy vehicle—the frontal armor of an M1 could not be penetrated by virtually any weapon Iraq had. McMaster knew this and put his strongest armor in the lead.

Being true to his word that he would lead from the front when it came time to engage the enemy, McMaster put his tank at the center of the formation and arrayed his two-tank platoons in a "V" formation echeloned to his right and left. Once in formation, he continued toward the suspected enemy locations. As his tank treads began to crest the backside of a small hill, he discovered he was nearly face-to-face with eight Iraqi T72 tanks.

The M1 tank, while on the move, can hit a pinpoint target from three miles away. That was the optimal engagement range because few Iraqi tanks could accurately fire to half that distance. McMaster, however, found himself within a couple hundred *yards* from the enemy, well within their lethal range. Immediately, he ordered his gunner to engage the closest tank while he simultaneously got on the troop command network and screamed, "Contact! Tanks direct front!"

There was only time to react. McMaster's tank had one round loaded in the barrel and ready to fire. The gunner squeezed the trigger before the commander's words had left his mouth and the first enemy vehicle exploded in a hail of fire and sparks.

McMaster's gunner then yelled out the type of shell he wanted and the young adrenaline-filled soldier in the turret had it in the breach within three seconds and ready to fire. Shifting immediately to the nearest target, the gunner yelled, "On the way!" and another 120mm sabot round was screaming at 2,000 meters per second, slamming into the second T72, producing yet another massive explosion.

Without waiting for any more instructions from McMaster, the gunner again yelled for an armor-piercing round, and another three seconds after that, a third Iraqi T72 tank was shredded. The resulting explosion was so massive it ripped the turret off the tank and sent it spinning into the air like a toy.

Similar scenes were taking place among the tanks to McMaster's left and right. The battle drills we had conducted so repetitively for years in training called for the platoon on the right to observe the first enemy tank exploding and then attack the next enemy target on its left, and for the tank platoon on the left to do likewise on its side. The effect was spectacular: Within eight seconds of first contact, eight Iraqi tanks were on fire. Not one of those first eight tanks had been able to get off a single shot in response.

Relieved of the immediate threat to his front, McMaster returned to the radio and began giving instructions to the remainder of the troops' tanks and scouts, and the attack continued with great ferocity. I was positioned between the leftmost tank and the rightmost CFV and used the M60 machine gun mounted on my commander's hatch to saturate everything between the tank and the CVF with 7.62 mm bullets.

As the attack continued, we realized that because of the sandstorm, we had been unable to locate the enemy vehicles before contact, and had driven directly into what might otherwise have been a trap. The Iraqi defense was surprisingly well-designed: They had tanks dug into the ground where only part of the turret was visible in some areas, designed to draw us into a killing zone where they believed they would get clear shots at us as we drove the three or four kilometers in the open.

Unfortunately for them, because of the ferocity of the sandstorm, they had neither seen nor heard our armored vehicles approaching and were not ready for the fight. Many of the crews were huddled *under* their tanks. Because they were unaware we were even there, when Red 6 destroyed the first tank, the Iraqi gunners thought they were being attacked *from the air*.

The Iraqi Republican Guards had been subjected to air attack from the coalition an average of once every 10 hours every day for more than a month. Their normal procedure during an air raid was to get out of the tank and hide under it to protect from our fighter-bombers (because it was more survivable than remaining in the turret).

By the time they realized where the attack was coming from, the Iraqi gunners were in a full panic and tried desperately to jump into their turrets to return fire. As our tanks blasted our way through their first line of defense, the Iraqis hastily returned fire with machine guns and tank direct fire with their 125mm cannons.

But we were already amid their defenses, and once panic has set in among troops in contact, it is incredibly difficult to regain the composure necessary to accurately aim and fire a tank. It was doubly difficult when the Iraqi crewmen saw their fellow soldiers being blasted to pieces on all sides. To me, the extraordinary scenes playing out in front of me reminded me—even then—of something I'd seen in movies.

As a boy growing up in Texas, I had often watched old World War II movies with John Wayne, George C. Scott, and Paul Newman. One particular scene from one memorable movie, however, had always captured my imagination, even as a kid. It was from the movie 'Patton.'

Near the end of the movie, Patton's armored division was racing across Europe and one battalion came into a pitched tank fight with a German panzer battalion in a night fight. It was wildly chaotic, with U.S. and Wehrmacht troops mixed together, tanks firing in both directions, machine guns, and artillery rounds exploding all around. But on that cold February day in 1991, I was now *living* the scene.

When Eagle Troop blasted through the enemy tank battalion's first line of defense, as McMaster and I had previously decided, I left my position with the scout platoon and got behind the lead tank section on the left. I was engaging anything that moved with the machine gun on my armored vehicle, watched as M1 tanks were firing their huge M50 machine guns and ear-shattering sound of their 120mm main guns firing at enemy tanks, watching the latter explode in hails of sparks and flames.

A dug-in Iraqi ammo bunker that an Eagle Troop tank had just destroyed.

Iraqi tanks and other armored vehicles were likewise chaotically firing back with their cannons and machineguns, trying to kill us. Iraqi infantrymen on the ground used rifles and AK-47 machine guns in a suicidal attempt to engage our tanks, but the bullets bounced harmlessly off our armor. Virtually none of the Iraqi infantrymen would survive the day.

Although the entire battle was to last until well after midnight and take nearly eight hours to complete, the first 23 minutes were as intense and wild as any human endeavor could ever be. In the days and weeks that would follow this major battle, I would see the horrors and utter devastation of the war, especially on the hapless civilians who suffered the most.

That is the reason why today I am a fierce advocate for diplomacy and settling conflicts short of war; the cost is devastatingly high – and permanent in its consequences. But that realization would only come later, after years of contemplation; on the night of Feb. 23, 1991. In the meantime, I still had fighting to do.

It had been drilled into us during our days of training in Europe that if you were caught in an enemy kill zone, you must *never* stop but continue the attack through their rear defenses, pausing to consolidate only after you are no longer in direct danger. We had made it through the first belt of Iraqi troops, but there were still tanks in front of us.

After destroying the first line of Iraqi defense, however, regimental headquarters ordered our squadron to stop and establish a hasty defense at a map grid known as the 70 Easting. Macgregor would not consider it, knowing for certain that to comply with that order would give the enemy a chance to recover from their shock. We would also still be in direct firing range of Iraqi weapons.

Our higher headquarters had been taken by as much surprise as we had been. To be fair, they also didn't know for sure what was still in front of us and were afraid of the squadron advancing too deeply into an enemy armored kill zone where we theoretically could be surrounded and annihilated. But when leaders in higher headquarters are operating in the blind, unaware of what's going on at the point of contact, they have to trust their junior officers—who *are* in direct contact—to do the right thing. That's what Macgregor did.

Once Eagle Troop's tank force had destroyed all the enemy armor as far as their thermal sights could observe, McMaster ordered a halt to the advance three kilometers farther than headquarters had requested. That was the 73 Easting, the map plot used to name the battle.

Once there, he ordered the troop to form a "goose egg" defensive perimeter with the tanks facing toward the last known enemy positions and the two platoons of Bradleys arrayed along the left and right to provide flank security. Macgregor then ordered Ghost Troop to come alongside our right flank and form a new forward line for the squadron.

Meanwhile, McMaster directed me to move back and pick up the two armored mortar vehicles and bring them forward so they could set up to fire as far forward of our position as possible to interdict any attempted enemy counterattack. Once I had chosen a good spot for them, I returned to my position just behind McMaster's tank. My primary job in the cavalry was to provide long-range fires in support of the commander so he could focus on the fight to his direct front.

Lt. Davis with fellow crewmember SPC Michael Orth alongside his armored fire support vehicle, Saudi Arabia December 1991

My vehicle was equipped with a powerful set of optics that could be hydraulically erected to allow me to see with pinpoint accuracy up to 10 kilometers ahead in both day and night. But, in keeping with things not working out after enemy contact, the hydraulics malfunctioned and would not allow the optics to be employed. Instead, I had to stand on top of my vehicle and use old-fashioned binoculars or, later, assist a nearby Bradley in using his thermal sights to get targeting data for the mortars when we began taking fire from infantrymen in a nearby trench.

For the next several hours, things in my sector settled down, as we had destroyed all the enemy troops in front of us. To my left, however, our sister troop, Ghost Troop, was just starting to fight. They fought a ferocious battle, using a combination of both direct fire from tanks and indirect fires from our howitzer battery and troop mortar crews.

After watching the battle to my left and events to my front for several hours, I noticed many of the vehicles attacking Ghost Troop were coming from several kilometers in front of our position, hidden from view by a slight depression in the terrain. Our tanks can only shoot what they can see, and even then, to a maximum of four kilometers. This area, which I suspected to be an enemy base camp, was at least six kilometers away.

As regimental headquarters was preparing to pass the fight on to the 1st Infantry Division, Macgregor wanted to make sure it was safe for them beyond the range of our tanks. He authorized me to conduct a trial artillery strike at the suspected base. At first, I requested a relatively small volley. Watching through my binoculars from atop my vehicle, I could see several secondary explosions when the rounds landed, indicating there were indeed vehicles there.

Macgregor then authorized one last major strike to include all the artillery cannons and rocket launchers in our area against the suspected Iraqi base camp. We fired more than 300, 155 mm artillery rounds and 12 rockets at an area more than three kilometers wide and one

Doug Macgregor's tank at the 73 Easting, February 1991

kilometer deep. It was the most amazing display of firepower I had ever seen. Before this battle, all I had done was call for fire using training rounds in small concentrations at Germany's Grafenwoehr Training Center. Seeing this massive demonstration now was astonishing (and, frankly, made me feel genuine sorrow for the Iraqi soldiers under barrage).

At sunrise the next morning and we could see the results of the battle, we counted more than 200 enemy dead. Eagle Troop and other 2nd Squadron units had destroyed an entire brigade of an Iraqi armored

35

division, including dozens of tanks and scores of other armored vehicles and military trucks.

The next morning there was a putrid smell that has been permanently seared into my memory: it was the obnoxious aroma created by the combination of the burning vehicles and the flesh of their former occupants.

Because it was winter, the Iraqi troops were wearing heavy coats. After the battle, I remember seeing three dead men who had been manning a machine gun in a bunker. One of the men was missing his head from the lower jaw up, and his two companions lay on his chest. I thought it perverse and yet somehow serene that, because I couldn't see the wounds through their coats, the other two men appeared to be peacefully sleeping.

War is a horrifying, brutish, and destructive undertaking. I have radically different memories of Desert Storm compared to most Americans—and most U.S. troops who participated, too. On the one hand, thankfully, neither I nor any of my personal friends were killed or wounded. We all made it home to our families safe and sound. Other American units—including Ghost Troop on my immediate left—were not so lucky and lost many of their friends.

Lt. Mike Hamilton, posing with a T55 tank he had destroyed the day before, February 27, 1991

36

Yet, on the other hand, I remember seeing the bodies of Iraqi troops after the battle laying in the dirt, appearing to have as little value as the wrecked tanks and mangled trucks burning next to them. I was deeply moved by the shell-shocked faces of the surviving Iraqi soldiers we took prisoner the next day. None of them had wanted to fight; none of them wanted to waste their lives for the arrogance of Saddam Hussein.

The Battle of 73 Easting was a great victory by the U.S. Army, validating the critical importance of having great leaders, solid institutional training, and premier combat equipment. We must always bear in mind, however, the permanent cost that war imposes on both the victors and the vanquished.

Chapter 3: *There's a Better Way to Do Business (The Army's Future Combat System)*

Barely was the confetti swept up from the New York City <u>ticker-tape parade</u> celebrating the Desert Storm victory before senior Pentagon leaders began designing the military of the future. Forward-thinking leaders don't stand on their laurels but ponder what's next; visionary leaders make it happen.

The Iraqi military we dispatched with such ease in 1991 had been the fifth-largest standing army in the world, but we knew even at the time that it had been a paper tiger, led by political appointees with little to no military capabilities, and manned by ill-trained and wholly unmotivated soldiers. The next battle foe America might face could be a capable, motivated, and modern force like that of China or Russia or even the less technologically capable (but still large and lethal) military of North Korea.

It takes upwards of a decade under the best of circumstances to reform and retool a modern military, and during the time of transition, they will endure periods of relative weakness. Thus, the ideal conditions to overhaul our military would be when the risk of unexpected attack by a capable foe would be at its lowest. That is exactly what existed in the mid-1990s.

We had just dismantled Saddam's Iraq and we knew he would not be an invasion risk in the region for the foreseeable future. The once-mighty Red Army of the Soviet Union had melted away with the <u>dissolution of the USSR</u> in 1992, and the Chinese Army was still a <u>pre-modern conscript-based force</u> that would be challenged to defend its borders, much less attack anyone else. This was the perfect time to reform the Department of Defense to posture us for military dominance well into the future.

Unfortunately, we botched the opportunity.

Flawed Foundations from the Beginning

U.S. Army leaders began what would be a years-long process of imagining the future of warfare and trying to design an American force that would be successful in that future.

It was a logical intent and could have produced something of great value for the country. Unfortunately, however, victory has a nasty habit of puffing up the egos of the victors, making them all too often think more highly of themselves than warranted. That's what happened to the Army's efforts almost from the beginning.

The speed with which the U.S. coalition dismantled Saddam's once-feared Republican Guard armored divisions left many Army leaders with the impression that swift victory had come because of inherent mental superiority on their part. We crushed Iraq in the air and on the ground in 1991 mostly because of their gross incompetence. That's not to say our armed forces weren't excellent at the time, however.

The quality and professional excellence of our soldiers and combat leaders in 1991, combined with then-outstanding military technology, sealed the outcome before the first tank round had been fired. But in Desert Storm's aftermath, too many of the Army's senior leaders believed their flattering press and overestimated their abilities. Taking risks by thinking outside the box and imagining new concepts and battle formations that don't yet exist is a good idea. But visionary thinking has to remain connected to reality.

The fatal flaw of the Army's leaders during this phase was their desire to make the future force look like something out of a blockbuster movie: they envisioned fantastic capabilities and then projected that vision on a world in which their fantasies would be a reality.

They ascribed technology to our future force that didn't exist, envisioned unrealistically high levels of intelligence and skills for our troops, while imaging we would face an enemy force that was antiquated, unimaginative, and entirely predictable (say, exactly like the Iraqi enemy we had vanquished so easily).

What they should have done was start with the expectation we would someday face a strong, capable, creative, and unpredictable enemy and then conceived of a future American force that could defeat it. They should have examined any and all technological development in our country, assessed many of the most promising ideas, and then adjusted the emerging doctrines and force development to match extant technologies that worked, leaving behind those that didn't.

Instead, they assumed all their ideas would come to fruition and they would develop all the technologies they desired merely by throwing enough money at them. They settled on doctrines and force structure without regard to whether the technology worked; they never changed their depiction of a weak, simple future enemy. Such wishful thinking doomed our efforts from the beginning.

My First Direct Engagement with the Future Force

When Desert Storm ended and the USSR disappeared, the U.S. no longer needed an Army with 750,000 troops and so embarked on a massive reduction in force which would ultimately see it shrink by an eye-popping quarter of a million men. Tens of thousands of soldiers would be forced out of the Army to meet the lower-end strength.

Serving in the Army was something I loved doing. I had no desire to leave. But the Army had different plans for me (and about 6,000 of my fellow lieutenants), and by the summer of 1994, I was a civilian.

I tried many times in the next few years to get back on to active duty, but the doors were all barred. What I could do, I soon discovered, was join the Individual Ready Reserves so I would at least be able to compete for short-term active tours for the Army's specific and temporary missions.

These tours could be as brief as 30 days or as long as nine months. In early 1997, while serving on a limited tour in South Korea, I was offered an amazing opportunity by a military legislative aide named David Davis (a retired Army colonel) to come work for him on the Washington staff of U.S. Sen. Kay Bailey Hutchison of Texas.

I was thrilled beyond description. Having the chance to go to the nation's capital and work for such a distinguished and powerful leader as Senator Hutchison was an opportunity for which I was most eager. Hutchison (the U.S. ambassador to NATO as of this writing) was the fourth-ranking Republican in the Senate when I joined the staff and an outspoken advocate for many of the policies I already supported.

Davis with fellow staffer for Sen. Kay Bailey Hutchison, Washington, 1998

Later that year, I attended my first congressional staff delegation trip to Fort Hood, Texas, to observe the Army's "Digital Division" in action at what they called the Advanced Warfighter Experiment. The purpose of the visit was for the Army to showcase what it claimed was a dramatic advancement in technology and capability compared to our force during Desert Storm. I was excited to see first-hand how the service had progressed since last I fought in a combat unit. What I observed, however, was something rather different from what the Army claimed.

When we arrived, Army escorts took our group of Senate aides to a field site where many tents were set up to replicate a division headquarters operating in a forward combat location. When I first arrived I was excited: the classic smell of Army tent material, the buzz of soldiers running everywhere, and a few armored vehicles parked around the perimeter made me remember my service in the 2nd ACR (and wish I were still serving in uniform). Once the briefings began, however, and various leaders explained what was being portrayed, my excitement quickly evaporated.

The Army representatives claimed that this Advanced Warfighter Experiment "proved" that technological advances now allowed combat units to be more lethal in combat with fewer troops and resources than in Desert Storm. They showed computer screens that depicted how a "digital division"—in this case, the 4th Infantry Division outfitted with impressive-looking new technology—could perform dramatically better than a "legacy division" of the Desert Storm era. Because of my direct combat experience in armored units and years spent maneuvering around the German countryside, I knew what they were showing was grossly inaccurate.

In a report I wrote for my immediate supervisor upon my return, I explained what we were being told and why it was a sham. The congressional aides who attended the event and had never served in the military came to the exact conclusion the event's organizers intended. The aides were wowed by the visuals, impressed by the sharp-looking soldiers all around them, and intimidated by the gruff-sounding generals lauding the system—and believed that everything they saw was real. I was the only Senate aide at the event who had combat experience of the type presented in the simulations, and I knew it was a fraud.

Some of the obvious flaws in the design of the simulation, I wrote to my boss, were that they were using software to wargame the battle that didn't have the capacity to project battle outcomes: It basically spit out the answer the modelers dictated, which was a massive U.S. win against what they claimed to be a powerful Russian-style opponent. Here is the most damning part of my report:

> *The scenario driving this experiment depicted the 4th ID initially performing a covering force mission across a frontage of 250km. Then they defended a sector 150km in width when the Corps was fully deployed. While in this defense, 4th ID absorbed a Russian-style combined arms army of **three divisions** and held. At the end of the battle the U.S. division*

strength was estimated to be between 50-55 percent. The simulators then depicted the 4th ID as immediately enduring a second attack, this time by a Russian tank army - again they repelled the attackers without allowing a penetration anywhere in sector.

In the 48-72 hours following the successful defense, the simulation depicted the 4th ID receiving replacements for the 45 percent to 50 percent of the U.S. troops that had been killed and wounded and were brought back to 90 percent strength. They then launched a complicated attack to destroy the remnants of both the combined arms army and the tank army...

To even suggest that any division could sustain 50 percent casualties and then receive replacements that had never trained with the division and expect them to conduct a successful attack within days is absolute fiction.

What they represent here is sheer Hollywood fantasy. Unless the enemy was worse than Saddam Hussein's troops, those things would never happen. But what concerns me, is they are clearly trying to give the impression that their success in the simulation battle proves they can reduce combat power and still get the job done.

My fears about what the Army intended to make the public believe was confirmed one month later. The *Army Times* newspaper ran a headline on Dec. 15 that read, "On track: Future force proves itself more lethal." The story quoted the general in charge of the modernization program making an astounding claim: "Look at the results of this exercise," the general said. "This one division...in simulation killed six divisions—two combined arms armies—in the first four days [with] considerably less losses than current divisions do."

I knew with 100 percent certainty the claims of such combat success were pure fiction. No one who had ever been in combat (or has studied modern military history) would believe something so fanciful. Two years later, however, my assessment was proven by the commander of the 4th ID Digital Division.

In March 1999, then-Colonel Rick Lynch commanded the 1st Brigade of the 4th Infantry Division (designated the "Digital Division") and led it through a tactical exercise at the National Training Center in California. In a June 2001 paper for the Institute for Defense Analysis, he wrote:

> *People are touting that information technology is going to show an immediate impact on our ability to conduct warfighting. They are trying to convince the world that information technology will show immediate improvements in lethality, survivability, and the ability to manage the tempo of the battle. But after hearing all these pronouncements, we then conduct a major test and these so-called improvements are not obvious.*

Lynch referred to a July 1999 Government Accountability Office report, "*Battlefield Automation.*" Mirroring what he had observed, the GAO investigators concluded that "the efforts thus far designed to measure force effectiveness have produced inconclusive results, with maneuver units in the field showing no significant increase in lethality, survivability, and operational tempo while modeling and simulation do show increases."

These multiple assessments, some of which came from the most senior field commanders in the program, should have led the Army's senior leaders back to the drawing board or at least to make major adjustments to the program. Instead, they arrogantly ignored the warnings and doubled down on the disaster-in-the-making.

"Army After Next"

In the spring of 1998, the Army, then two years into an effort to reform itself under the banner of then-Chief of Staff General Dennis Reimer's "Army After Next" agenda, conducted the third in a series of simulated wargames to ascertain the validity of a new warfighting construct. AAN was expressly designed to provide the existing Army with a long-term vision for what the service would eventually become "well into the next century" and, most critically, to "ensure that this vision informs evolving Army research and development requirements."

The concept of experimenting with new ideas, combining both computer and field exercises, was sound. Doing so would give the Army's senior leaders a chance to either validate ideas as sound or expose them as inadequate. A failed test in and of itself is not a bad thing, because knowing what won't work is often as important as knowing what will. It is essential, however, to have the intellectual honesty and moral courage to acknowledge when one's cherished preconceptions are revealed to be inadequate and to continue making adjustments until you find something that does work.

Had the Army taken this approach (which, it should be pointed out, it largely did when developing the M1 Abrams Tank, the Bradley Fighting Vehicle, and the Apache Attack Helicopter in the 1970s and 80s), we would certainly have a materially more modern and capable force than the one we have today, which is only incrementally better than the one we had 30 years ago.

Unfortunately, Army leaders chose to hide or ignore any failure and continued forward with their preferred concepts even when they proved utterly ineffective. Even with the previous rounds of failure, the senior leadership had what might have been their best chance to do the right thing in the major computer-simulated wargame that took place in 1998.

The RAND Corporation's Arroyo Center was tasked by the Army to chronicle the event and write a summary of results upon completion. In its report, "Issues Raised During the Army After Next Spring Wargame," and as the GAO had done in previous efforts, RAND identified significant weaknesses.

The Army After Next forces depicted in the simulated conflict, "were clearly unsuited for urban operations," the report explained. "Its tilt-rotor (aircraft) and light armored vehicles were very vulnerable to enemy fire coming from concealed locations such as buildings.

Also, the precision-guided munitions (PGMs) and information systems of the Battle Force were seriously degraded in the city." After detailing a long list of specific tactical shortcomings portrayed in the event, the authors concluded by noting that previous wargames "tended to demonstrate advantages of the current... concept, while the Spring Wargame [of 1998] tended to demonstrate limitations." They observed, in other words, that the then-existing force was shown to be *better* than the simulated future concept.

The report also noted, "The Army needs to develop and examine other concepts for its future forces." And most ominously, RAND warned that while the Army may ultimately conclude its future concepts are good, "it cannot make an informed decision without examining alternatives."

I cannot say whether Army leadership considered other alternatives behind closed doors, as I had neither direct knowledge of their deliberations nor access to sources that did. Based on what happened in the three or four years following, however, I can confidently say any such alternatives were abandoned and their original ideas—which had now been *proven* as a failure in three major simulations—continued without being materially altered.

The year after the AAN Wargame, General Eric Shinseki replaced Reimer as the Army's chief of staff, and in testimony before the Senate Appropriations Committee on March 6, 2002, he shared his vision for modernization.

During the previous three years, the general said, the Army had taken a "hard and discriminating" look at itself. After examining the Army's capability against the emerging strategic environment, he told the committee, "we decided to take some risk, to break with our past. We committed ourselves to transforming the way we will fight and will win the wars, the new wars of this new century." The lynchpin of that modernization program, he told members of Congress, was the Future Combat Systems.

The Army was soon to designate a lead systems integrator to build the FCS to "accelerate transformation to the Objective Force by the year

2010." In the September/October 2000 edition of *Military Review*, Shinseki specified that the objective force he envisioned would be able to "put combat force anywhere in the world in 96 hours after lift-off," and "build that capability into a momentum that generates a warfighting division on the ground in 120 hours and five divisions in 30 days."

While all that sounds terrific on briefing slides (what country wouldn't love to have this ability?) the technology necessary and the physical infrastructure that would be required to transport five divisions in 30 days did not then exist. Shinseki committed the U.S. to pursuing this strategy, though there was no proof such technology would ever materialize. It is amazing to consider that before knowing or testing the technology necessary to produce the Army that the chief of staff envisioned, he had fully committed the service to the course of action.

I am a strong advocate of taking prudent risk by pushing the envelope to try to make things better. When it comes to military technology and strategies, nations and armies can't afford to rest on past glory and assume they will always remain on top—opponents are constantly gunning to develop the next big thing that will neutralize their opponent's strengths. But neither can we be foolhardy and shoot for the stars, *assuming* we'll get there without having first done the hard and tedious work of validating the new ideas and hardware.

This hubris of assuming we'd succeed to our highest aspirations without having any evidence it would work proved devastating to our modernization efforts. In July 2005, just three years into the FCS program, I made my first public assessment of the system in the *Armed Forces Journal* and raised the first warning flag that we were headed in the wrong direction.

The United States military, I wrote, was the strongest, most advanced combat force on the planet. The Army's intent to stay that way well into the future was right, but "$4.6 billion and two years into the program, the FCS effort is further from it its target production date than when it started and its projected budget has ballooned from $92 billion to $125 billion." Aside from major budgetary and scheduling problems, however, I explained that the bigger problems were with the concept itself.

To achieve combat superiority and pull off Shinseki's goal of deploying a full division in 120 hours, the FCS had to reduce the weight of its tanks from 70 tons to 19 tons. The only way to do that would be to radically reduce the amount of protective armor, which would make the vehicles vulnerable to even the most antiquated armor systems of the weakest adversaries in the world.

The FCS designers claimed they would get around that problem by creating a network that would link multiple combat platforms throughout the battlespace, which would give U.S. forces near-perfect intelligence and allow them to engage enemy heavy armor without having to be in direct line of sight.

For FCS to work as designed, the Army would have to physically create the technology to link dispersed combat platforms over many kilometers of terrain, produce new armor that was strong enough to withstand enemy attacks yet light enough to meet standards, build a secure broadband communications network that could function in austere environments and withstand enemy attempts to block it. Besides these Herculean tasks, there were two major problems with the concept itself.

First, the FCS plan was predicating the security of our future force on the twin assumptions that we would have perfect intelligence and that enemy tanks and artillery would never find us on the battlefield. This was the height of wishful thinking. Anyone who has ever studied war knows that operations rarely go off as planned, that the enemy usually finds ways to attack in unexpected places, and that one's own side often makes mistakes.

The FCS was building a system that could only fight and survive if *everything worked perfectly all the time,* and that we would never fight a capable adversary.

Second, the program was predictably and routinely plagued by its inability to produce integral new technologies. Test after test exposed that the technology would not perform to the level needed to make the system function to standard, yet the leaders stubbornly refused to concede the failure, pressing forward regardless. The FCS was clearly leading us to a dangerous future. Fortunately, as I also pointed out in the 2005 article, superior alternatives were already available.

Douglas Macgregor, under whom I had fought more than a decade earlier in Desert Storm, published a book in 1997 that laid out a new modernization and reform plan that would improve the striking power of the Army called "Breaking the Phalanx: A New Design for Landpower in the 21st Century." Unlike the FCS program, which relied on unproven technology and discounted the possible actions of capable foes, "Breaking the Phalanx" ought to leverage *existing* technology, shedding unnecessary and redundant headquarters elements and reorganizing troops into "combat groups" that put a greater emphasis on striking power and mobility.

Regrettably, in the early 2000s, Army leaders were rigid and inflexible in pursuing the favored FCS program at all costs. And as events would continue to unfold in the coming years, it would indeed cost the U.S. a great deal while producing precisely zero for the nation's security.

Two years after writing my first FCS article in the Armed Forces Journal, I was given the chance to serve in the FCS program at its Fort Bliss, Texas, headquarters. I had hoped—naively, I'll now admit—that maybe I could help improve the system from within. What I didn't realize at the time, but would soon painfully find out, was the extent to which the Army's senior leadership was willing to go to protect their cherished Future Combat Systems concept.

Fort Bliss and the Future Combat Systems

After less than two years in Washington, I had returned to my native Texas to work as an operations manager for an alarm monitoring company in Dallas.

It was there that I watched TV screens in horror with my colleagues as our world was rocked by the terrorist attacks on Sept. 11, 2001. I felt an instant, irrepressible urge to return to the Army to be part of our nation's response. It took almost a year, but in late 2002 I was mobilized as a reserve officer back to active duty and served in the bowels of the Pentagon in the Army Operations Center, where I would watch as the Army's senior leaders orchestrated Operation Iraqi Freedom in 2003.

By mid-2005, the war in Iraq was spiraling out of control and the insurgency was beginning to blaze beyond our ability to control. The Department of Defense needed tens of thousands of additional active-duty troops to maintain the crush of combat deployments to both Iraq and Afghanistan, and before the end of the year, I had changed my branch from artillery to armor and been returned to full active service.

Now a major, my first assignment was with the Combined Forces Command, Afghanistan to serve as a liaison officer. I would split my time that year among CENTCOM headquarters in Tampa, Florida, CENTCOM-Forward in Qatar, and at CFC-A headquarters in Kabul (more on my experiences in Afghanistan in Chapter 4).

I went straight from Afghanistan to Germany in 2006, as I was assigned to be the second-in-command of the divisional cavalry squadron of the 1st Armored Division in Buedingen, Germany. As part of the Army's attempt to modernize, the cavalry unit was inactivated. After only 15 months, I was reassigned again, this time to the FCS program at Fort Bliss, Texas.

It didn't take long to discover that the same thing I'd observed the Army do with a single division at Fort Hood in 1997 when I was a Senate aide, was now being done on a significantly larger scale with FCS at Fort Bliss. Year after year the congressionally-mandated reports from the Government Accountability Office—all of which I read thoroughly— revealed significant problems and warned that the system was in danger of failing.

Each year the Army's senior leaders told members of Congress at hearings that the GAO didn't see the full picture: the program was actually on schedule, on budget, and headed for success. Almost from the beginning of my tenure in Fort Bliss, I had observed and taken part in demonstrations, experimentation, and computer simulations for the

FCS which demonstrated that, if anything, I had underestimated just how bad the program was and how unlikely it was to ever succeed.

At first, I tried to offer my recommendations for improvement to the organization's leaders, going through the chain of command by writing confidential memorandums. In November 2007, I sent an official memorandum to my immediate boss, a full colonel, in response to a simulation exercise in which I had taken part a few days earlier. During this exercise, I had been role-playing a company commander using some of the technology FCS had planned to distribute to the current force in the near future.

The scenario unfolded in a Middle Eastern village similar to those I had seen with the 2nd ACR in Iraq, so I had some idea how things might have played out in a real-life battle. I was concerned from the beginning because the software used to model the simulation was the wrong type. As with the Advanced Warfighter Experiment at Fort Hood a decade earlier, it could not accurately show the results of a force-on-force battle.

In one simulated battle, the software depicted an enemy fighter hiding in a mud-walled house and firing an AK-47 machine gun from a window at a U.S. armored vehicle. His fire disabled the vehicle (as I observed in Desert Storm, bullets from AK-47s will harmlessly bounce off most armored vehicles), yet when that same vehicle fired back at the shooter, the game recorded no effect.

If a U.S. combat vehicle had fired a burst from its 50-caliber machine gun against the house, it would have sliced "through the mud walls like butter, killing or suppressing the enemy," I wrote in a memo to my boss. "In the game...no friendly weapon system could penetrate either a window or a wall." The result, I concluded, "was that tactics were used in the simulation that would never have been used in real life, leading exercise officials to draw faulty conclusions."

I raised these concerns with my boss because when the simulation officials submitted the results of the computer games to the FCS commanding general, I feared the tactics portrayed would "be characterized as being doctrinally sound, that we used tactics representative of how

[U.S. combat units] units would actually fight, and that the use and utility of [FCS] items was accurately represented. It is my view that none of those things are true."

The colonel dismissed my concerns and told me the general was smarter than I gave him credit for. Mere weeks later my concerns were confirmed.

I was in the back row of the conference room when those very officials made their report to the general, and they reported almost verbatim what I had feared. Whether the general was smart or not, when the experts reported that a computer simulation had "proven" the effectiveness of the FCS technology in something representing "a real-life situation," he believed it—and passed that happy result up the Army chain of command. Those leaders would, in turn, later report to Congress and others of the alleged "successes" I had *directly observed* to be in error.

After this and other attempts to go through the chain of command to raise my concerns, I decided to escalate to another course of action. I was already publishing military and foreign policy articles in various outlets, so I decided to write a new one on the FCS and again send it to the Armed Forces Journal. Not wanting to just throw rocks at a problem and complain, I decided to focus most of my efforts on recommendations on how to make the system better.

By the end of 2007, I had completed a detailed 42-page analysis of the Army's modernization efforts, identified the problems in detail, and offered a roadmap for how to modernize effectively. The AFJ would publish my 4,000-word essay in its January 2008 edition titled *Heavy & Agile: Nine Steps to a More Effective Force*. I finished the draft of both over Thanksgiving Weekend, pulling no punches in the opening:

> *The Department of Defense (DoD) is modernizing and transforming itself into a force designed to dominate all challengers in any future battle… While some components of DoD's efforts are outstanding and promise significant advantage to future American forces, other elements are so far off the mark that if remedial actions are not taken, American*

forces could suffer a significant battlefield defeat in future war—a defeat that might otherwise be avoidable.

Not wishing to take anyone by surprise, on Nov. 25 I sent the draft of the full document to many of the leaders of the program, several Pentagon generals, and the executive officer of the secretary of the Army. "Since I'm certain none of you agrees with all the opinions I shared in this work," I wrote, "I wanted to make sure you were fully aware of all that would be in the report before it is published early next year."

I also offered them all the chance to "make sure that I have not characterized" incorrectly the conversations I had with them in the past and that my words "accurately reflect your opinion on the matter discussed." I sent it to 27 men and women, including the three-star general in charge of the Army Capabilities Integration Center, the higher headquarters for the FCS program.

I got a few replies from some of them, mostly courteous and polite. On Dec. 7, the executive officer for the secretary of the Army said it was "awesome" and that he was "glad" I was publishing my report. After having heard nothing from the three-star general, in mid-December I wrote his aide and asked what he thought of it. The general had read it while on a recent flight, the aide wrote back to me, and said the general had found it "interesting" but then handed the paper back to the aide without further comment.

Other than this feedback, during the nearly two months between the time I'd sent my draft to that large group and the time it was published in the *AFJ*, I had barely heard a word from anyone. I suspect that most or all of these leaders disregarded my work as coming from some obscure Army major and didn't give it a second thought—until, that is, it went live online in January 2008.

Then all hell broke loose.

As I would discover in the following months from officers with direct knowledge, there were at least four generals in the Pentagon who were furious beyond description. They immediately called lower-ranking generals and colonels of the FCS program—including the one-star overseeing our program—and, I was told, explained in no uncertain terms that I should be silenced. An officer who was in the room during a heated exchange told me that the one-star general demanded my direct supervisor punish me in some way.

To his credit, my boss, who was also a combat veteran, demonstrated considerable moral courage and point-blank refused. How could he punish me, he asked, when I had followed protocol and given the command two full months to view the work? After a few moments of silence, I was told, the general then said to my boss, "Fine, then Davis no longer works for you. He works for someone else now." I was taken out of my job and placed in another section of the FCS program far away from any direct engagement in experimentation or field demonstration activities.

My new boss, also a full colonel, apparently had ambitions to become a general, because he enthusiastically obeyed the general's intent for me. He made my life a living hell. No one could take any overt action to punish me because I had clearly violated no regulations and had in fact suggested practical ways the Army could improve the modernization efforts.

But they could—and my new boss did—make my life miserable, condemning me for failing to follow instructions to the letter (sometimes accusing me of failure even when I'd precisely complied), belittling me in front of other soldiers, falsely accusing me of failing at some tasks the colonel knew I had never been assigned, and regularly condemning me – viciously, in some cases, for things that never even happened.

It worked. After my first boss put himself on the line by refusing to take negative action against me, no one else dared stick their neck out for me. I was on my own, at the mercy of this new colonel. Out of self-preservation, I went silent, kept my mouth shut, and wrote nothing for the rest of my assignment at Fort Bliss.

The only way I was able to escape the mental hell was, perversely, going back to combat. I was able to convince my career manager at the armor branch to pull me from the assignment early and send me to Iraq as the team chief of a group of military experts training an Iraqi border battalion. I left Fort Bliss in late 2008 to begin training at Fort Riley, Kansas, for a 2009 deployment.

During the rest of my "banishment" at Fort Bliss, however, the FCS program continued to founder. With every test failure, the command's senior leaders made more excuses to congressional leaders and government watchdogs, explaining away shortcomings, covering up other failures, and outright claiming some aspects of the program succeeded when they had failed. Senior FCS leaders had succeeded in silencing me, but they could not hide the program failures forever.

FCS Conclusion

The results of our senior leaders' willingness to prevent Congress from knowing the truth about FCS eventually cost the U.S. close to a decade of lost development opportunity and nearly $20 billion (to date, even the follow-up programs to FCS have likewise failed to produce so much as a single functioning prototype). In large measure we are, in terms of force composition, technologically at the same place we were after Desert Storm; we are decades behind where we could have been by now—where we by all rights ought to be.

The most direct consequence was the death of the FCS program itself. On April 6, 2009, Secretary of Defense Robert Gates canceled the heart of the program, the new armored vehicles, and the full FCS program would be canceled the following month. Gates justified the cancelation by citing many of the very shortcomings I had identified in my FCS articles and analysis papers.

"I have concluded that there are significant unanswered questions concerning the FCS vehicle design strategy," he explained. "I am also concerned that, despite some adjustments, the FCS vehicles—where lower weight, higher fuel efficiency, and greater informational awareness are expected to compensate for less armor—do not adequately reflect the lessons of counterinsurgency and close-quarters combat in Iraq and Afghanistan."

Our potential adversaries, meanwhile, made considerable progress in closing the once-enormous capability gap between their militaries and ours. The clearest example, which should be the most embarrassing to the U.S., has been the creation and production of the <u>Russian Armata Universal Combat Platform</u>. The FCS was designed to be a "system of systems" using a common chassis among 8 different ground combat vehicles, including a mobile tank-like vehicle and an infantry carrier, none of which ever materialized.

Meanwhile, the Russians needed only six years to design, test, and start producing technologically advanced combat vehicles, highlighted by the Armata T-14 tank and T-15 personnel carrier. Both employ <u>state of the art armor</u>, weapon systems, ammunition, and fire control systems—and all feature a common chassis. The T-14 in particular appeared to be just as durable and deadly as the U.S. Abrams tank. In 1991, the Abrams could have won a tank-on-tank engagement against possibly every potential enemy tank in the world.

That advantage has been lost.

The U.S. had every advantage imaginable following our historic tactical victory over Iraq in 1991. We had the world's most powerful ground, air, and sea forces, the world's greatest economy, and the horizon was clear of likely conflicts for the foreseeable future. The USSR had collapsed after the end of the Cold War, and Russia was weak and unstable. China was decades away from producing a modern force. The late 1990s were the perfect time to reform and rebuild our military to remain dominant well into the 21st century.

But we failed, utterly, to take advantage of that opportunity, primarily owing to the hubris and unbridled arrogance of our top uniformed and civilian leadership. We shot for the stars but weren't willing to do the hard work necessary to reach them. We set properly high goals but weren't willing to modify them when our initial plans didn't succeed. When people identified the errors—and I was far from the only one to do so—they were ignored and the necessary adjustments were rejected in favor of the original fantasy.

We know for certain this avoidable failure has cost us tens of billions of dollars, two decades of potential modernization time, and the continual rebooting of technology that was first fielded in the early 1980s. Our potential enemies have advanced in abilities over the same timeframe and now rival our battlefield capabilities. The true cost of this failure, however, may only be known when we can look back from further into the future after we have suffered a bloody battlefield loss to an opponent who should never have had a chance.

Chapter 4: *Fighting Against the Taliban in Afghanistan – and Against U.S. Leaders in Washington*

Lt. Col. Davis, on patrol in the mountains adjacent to Afghan-Pakistan border, 2011

The first time the American public became aware I existed was in February 2012 when I was the subject of a *New York Times* expose written by Scott Shane that was published simultaneously with an explosive analysis I had written on the truth of the war in Afghanistan for the Armed Forces Journal. I had gone public, while still a lieutenant colonel on active duty in the Army, with this harsh truth: the Pentagon's senior civilian and uniformed leaders were systematically lying to the American people, claiming success in the war where the reality in Afghanistan was a perpetual failure.

I had been driven to take this action that placed my career in considerable jeopardy because the lies hadn't simply fooled the public; they directly led to <u>tens of thousands</u> of American troops being killed and wounded, <u>hundreds of thousands</u> suffering traumatic brain injuries and post-traumatic stress disorder, and <u>upwards of $6 trillion</u> squandered. By itself, deceiving the American public at such a profound cost was a powerful motivator. But because I had been warning of precisely this outcome for many years, my frustration was intolerable and drove me to action.

Before the Deployment

In February 2009, less than one month into office, President Obama got to work on one of his signature campaign promises—to win the "good war" in Afghanistan—by deploying 17,000 additional U.S. troops on top of the 38,000 already there. "This increase is necessary to stabilize a deteriorating situation in Afghanistan," <u>Obama declared</u>, "which has not received the strategic attention, direction, and resources it urgently requires."

In April 2009, while I was deployed in Iraq, I wrote an essay for the Armed Forces Journal provocatively titled, "<u>The Afghan mistake</u>." Based on my combat experience in Desert Storm and my first deployment to Afghanistan in 2005, I knew for sure that sending 17,000 more troops to Afghanistan would exacerbate, not help, the problem and would extend the war. Failure to honestly consider on-the-ground realities, I argued, would "perversely result in paying more to lose." Were the president willing "to consider an alternative [plan]," I added, he "could salvage the entire operation." I had solid reasons for this view.

Unless Obama was prepared to bring in overwhelming numbers of combat troops (probably more than 300,000) and commit to waging an existential battle to exterminate the Taliban from both Afghanistan and Pakistan, I emphasized, "adding another 12,000 or 30,000 troops will amount to trying to put out a house fire with a garden hose."

At the time we were winding down what would eventually be eight years of fruitless counterinsurgency war in Iraq in which we had deployed as many as 180,000 troops. There was no chance that Obama—who had campaigned against the Iraq war—was about to dramatically expand the nature of our war in Afghanistan and send that many troops there. What he would eventually do, however, was try to win a military victory on the cheap by sending in only a handful of troops to accomplish what even hundreds of thousands couldn't.

For very practical, fundamental reasons, it was clear to me even in early 2009 the U.S. could not win a military campaign by deploying more combat troops. At that time, peace in Afghanistan already was being prevented by a surging Taliban, remnants of al-Qaeda, provincial warlords operating on their own, drug kingpins, and common thugs. "This is a fight we can't win" I emphatically wrote, "given the current or projected level of commitment, and while this galls our Patton-esque passion for a clear-cut 'victory', changes are clearly required."

It was vitally important, I continued, that we reorient our efforts in Afghanistan and throughout the region in a way that acknowledged cultural and historical realities and would posture the U.S. and NATO to deal effectively with transnational terror groups that could theoretically pose legitimate strategic threats. If we failed to acknowledge these realities, however, we would "play to the strength of the enemy, plunge ourselves deeper into a fight that is potentially unwinnable, and for all our effort, find ourselves more strategically vulnerable than we were before we accepted battle."

This article marked the first time I had suggested the best course of action for the U.S. was to withdraw our combat forces from Afghanistan. I argued we should elevate the role of diplomacy and humanitarian assistance, provide some level of training and air support to the Afghan troops, and conduct counterterror operations that made sense for our security. This strategy included some risk, I acknowledged. It would be possible that the government of Afghan President Hamid Karzai could collapse and lead to a resurgence of fighting.

The negative consequences we risked suffering if we failed to withdraw, however, were higher than the potential benefit of trying to accomplish the unattainable. My concluding warning proved to be prescient. "But the hard question that must be asked:"

> *Would the collapse of the current government after the withdrawal of our main combat troops, however undesirable, be better or worse than increasing the number of American combat forces in Afghanistan and possibly keeping the government afloat—but at the cost of a continually strengthening Taliban and increasing the number of dead American soldiers and Afghan civilians?*

Of course, the White House did not take my advice and Obama did send the 17,000 troops to Afghanistan. Yet as I had predicted, that increase directly and quickly led to more U.S. casualties. The deterioration in the mission was so rapid that just months later, a leaked memo from U.S. commander Gen. Stanley McChrystal to Obama claimed the war could be lost in "the next 12 months" if we did not change strategy and dramatically increase the number of troops—upwards of 45,000.

The big change in strategy, McChrystal wrote in his extensive analysis, called for transitioning to a counterinsurgency mission focused on winning hearts and minds, and would thus require tens of thousands more troops. The jump from 38,000 to near 60,000 troops in the previous strategy was doomed to failure; in my view, almost tripling the number of troops we had at the beginning of 2009—and taking on an even more impossible task—guaranteed we'd lose.

Days later, I began to write an extensive analysis explaining why McChrystal's proposed strategy would be even less likely to succeed and offered a detailed alternative. At the time I was serving at the Defense Intelligence Agency in Washington, D.C. while recuperating from a medical issue.

I had been deployed from January 2009 until late May 2009 in Iraq serving as the team chief for a Military Training Team. As a major, I had led a group of 11 officers and senior enlisted soldiers, experts in select fields, into the Mason Province to train an Iraqi Border Battalion astride the Iraq/Iran border. In early May 2009, I began having some health problems that turned worse as the month progressed, to the point I had to be medically evacuated to the hospital at Fort Belvoir, Virginia (fortunately, near where my permanent residence was at the time).

I would undergo treatment for many months and later had shoulder surgery, but the latter part of my stay at Fort Belvoir was mainly to convalesce and regain my strength so I could return to duty. Because it was driving me crazy not to be doing the duties for which I had been trained, the Army allowed me to work for local units between doctor visits. I was very fortunate to get the assignment at the DIA.

Though my assignment called for me to focus on the European continent, my boss allowed me the freedom to begin writing a detailed report that would examine the pros and cons of the McChrystal proposal with the pros and cons of an alternative mission I would propose. It would be called _Go Big or Go Deep_.

In the paper, I argued the general's plan was so ambitious and so big as to be militarily unattainable. By comparison, my plan called for dramatically reducing the scope and scale of our operation and setting objectives that had a reasonable chance of success. McChrystal wanted to engage in a full-blown counterinsurgency war and I argued the president should scale back the mission to one focused on American national security based on counterterror operations.

The first third of the document analyzed the McChrystal plan and explained why it had little chance of success. The second section was devoted to detailing my alternative strategy of a counterterror-focused battle plan. The last major section examined the potential risk to the country of both plans. While I argued my plan had a better chance of success, I felt it important to honestly consider what might happen if we made the effort and it didn't work. I also outlined the risks of following the McChrystal plan. The risks in his plan were many and substantial:

- First, if the president agreed to McChrystal's troop increase, we would likely stoke anti-American and anti-foreigner impulses among the Afghan population, which would undercut our stated desire to win hearts and minds. At the same time, even

40,000 troops would be insufficient to pacify the entire country. With the troop levels envisioned, we would have too many to conduct an effective counterinsurgency operation of the type McChrystal envisioned and too few to conduct a military conquest operation.

- Trying to build an Afghan Army of 400,000 within the 18 months McChrystal promised would be an impossible task, as there was no existing experienced talent pool from which to draw. It would take a decade of sustained effort to produce even a minimally competent force.

- Having a competent government that its people trust and support is a core necessity for any counterinsurgency strategy to work. It was always clear that the risk of failed government would be high regardless of what plans Obama agreed to. But predicating our success on the Afghan government successfully eradicating corruption – within the 18 months McChrystal would be given – was an impossible task and would doom our efforts.

- By increasing the U.S. combat strength in Afghanistan by a full nine brigade combat teams, we would antagonize many citizens. These people, who would otherwise have no interest in attacking Americans, would undoubtedly turn into enemies, as we would be viewed as invading, foreign occupiers. Even the dedicated Taliban enemies would only have the capacity to attack U.S. troops if we sent them to Afghanistan – and give them a large number of known, fixed targets to attack the Taliban would otherwise not have.

And finally, perhaps most importantly:

- I argued it was clear from the beginning that McChrystal's Go Big plan would result in significant numbers of American combat troops remaining deployed in Afghanistan for another five to 10 years. The significance and difficulty of that cannot be casually dismissed: continued deployment of America's combat forces year after year with no end in sight will, at some point, create genuine damage to our core warfighting capabilities: too much focus on a counterinsurgency would diminish our ability to engage near-peer competitors such as China, Russia, or North Korea.

I finished _Go Big or Go Deep_ in October 2009 after having been promoted to lieutenant colonel a month earlier. I had read a news report in which Jay Carney, the communications director for Vice President Joe Biden, had been quoted making comments about Afghanistan that led me to believe Biden would be sympathetic to my views. If the vice president already had the right inclinations—and his views were in contrast to the much more hawkish views dominating the DC airwaves at the time—I thought perhaps armed with the info in my report, it could help him make his case during White House internal debates regarding the efficacy of McChrystal's request.

I don't know why I thought this was a good idea, but I decided to take a bold chance and contact Carney to offer him the document. I had no inside contacts at the time and merely went online and found the main switchboard number to the White House. I intended to call, be transferred to the vice president's press office, and when the receptionist answered, I hoped to be allowed to email the document to Carney.

I did have a lot of confidence in the quality of the document, however, and if the press secretary got hold of it, I believed there would be a chance he might like it. In any case, what did I have to lose? Things worked out quite differently than I had imagined.

I asked to be forwarded to the vice president's press office. To my shock, it wasn't a receptionist who answered the call, but Carney himself. After briefly introducing myself, I told him that based on my combat experience, I had written an assessment of McChrystal's proposal I thought he might find interesting. I told him it was an unclassified document based on open-source reporting, and though I was assigned to the DIA, this was my personal assessment. I did point out, however, that it was in sync with the comments he had just made. To my relief, he agreed without hesitation to allow me to email it to him.

Carney emailed me on Oct. 19, writing, "I did forward your report to the vice president's national security adviser, who said he found it very interesting. Since he is deeply involved in the discussions at the White House, you can be confident that your ideas have reached a high level. Where it goes from there is hard to say."

That began an association that would later include meetings at Caribou Coffee down the street from the White House, a private meeting with Biden's National Security Advisor Tony Blinken in his White House office, and the following January a meeting with Carney at Bagram Air Base in Afghanistan, where he facilitated a brief meeting for me with Biden. I told almost no one of this interaction, of course, and kept it absolutely quiet; I knew if

A photo Davis took on 28 April, 2011 of Jay Carney in his White House office while home on leave from Afghanistan.

anyone got wind of it in Army circles — or worse, in the media — such high-level access would end as would any future potential to influence policy.

As author Jonathan Alter would later describe in his book, "The Promise," at the time I sent this document, there was a major debate brewing in the White House between those advocating for surging 30,000 U.S. troops to expand the Afghan counterinsurgency strategy, and those arguing for a smaller footprint and limited mission.

The "surgers" were composed of heavyweight military and civilian leaders: Secretary of Defense Robert Gates, Secretary of State Hillary Clinton, Chairman of the Joint Chiefs of Staff Admiral Mike Mullen, and General David Petraeus. Leading the charge for restraint were Biden and Lt. Gen. Douglas Lute, Obama's coordinator for Afghanistan-Pakistan policy.

The cumulative prestige and heft of the surgers easily swamped Biden and Lute, and in the end, Obama chose not to go against Petraeus and company. If the president wouldn't be swayed by his vice president and a three-star general, he certainly wasn't going to listen to an obscure Army lieutenant colonel. On Dec. 1, 2009, Obama announced during a speech at West Point of his decision to surge.

"I have determined that it is in our vital national interest," the president told the cadets (as the rest of America watched on television), "to send an additional 30,000 U.S. troops to Afghanistan. After 18 months, our troops will begin to come home." Although Obama said the days "of providing a blank check" to military operations were over, it was clear to me even then that the mission he ordered would be almost impossible to accomplish with military means.

Obama said he ordered a "military strategy that will break the Taliban's momentum and increase Afghanistan's capacity over the next 18 months." Breaking the Taliban's "momentum" was a term Petraeus would use to great effect in public statements throughout the surge period. The problem is, it was not a military term, could be neither defined nor quantified, and it was therefore impossible for the public to know if the mission was a success or failure.

The second part of the mission, increasing Afghanistan's "capacity," was likewise impossible to quantify or measure. Again, with no metrics on which to base an assessment, no one could tell if the mission was succeeding brilliantly or failing miserably. As subsequent events would later expose, Petraeus played that ambiguity for all it was worth, telling Congress and the American people with conviction that we were succeeding.

By the summer of 2010, the first reports coming out of Afghanistan from Petraeus, now commander of Central Command, sounded optimistic. I had projected the risk of failure was high in my October 2009 analysis, but Petraeus and Undersecretary of Defense for Policy Michelle Flournoy testified at Congressional hearings in June that early reports out of Afghanistan were good.

"So far, we believe we have been making gradual but important progress," Flournoy said, and emphasized that "our overall assessment is that we are heading in the right direction in Afghanistan." Petraeus added that in the previous 18 months, the U.S. and NATO partners "have worked hard to get the inputs right in Afghanistan," and that this "hugely important" mission is "seeing early progress."

I was hopeful, then, that they were being proven right and I being proven wrong. Of course, it would be a little embarrassing for my assessment to have been proven inaccurate, but for them to be proven right would mean that the war could end soon and the bloodshed would stop. Protecting U.S. troops and preserving the lives of those who might later deploy was of great importance to me.

Initial Deployment in Late 2010

By early 2010, I had completed my medical rehabilitation and been assigned to the Rapid Equipping Force, based in Fort Belvoir, just outside Washington, DC. The assignment, to my great happiness, could require me to begin a one-year deployment to Afghanistan starting that November. If we were going to win the war, I wanted to be a part of it. It wouldn't take long, however, to discover just how inaccurate Petraeus and Flournoy had been at their hearing.

I arrived at Bagram Airbase in Afghanistan in November and spent the next month transitioning with the officer I was replacing. My job as REF Chief was to visit as many U.S. combat units in as many provinces as I could to find out what equipment they might need to successfully carry out their mission. My first official visit to a combat unit was in December to Ghazni Province where I went on a joint combat patrol with U.S. and Polish soldiers.

The Polish troops led the patrol, and I rode in one of their armored vehicles. The plan was to drive across the countryside through several villages, dismount and walk the main street of each village, then remount our vehicles to continue the route until we returned to the base camp later that night. As we approached the outskirts of the first village on our route, the vehicles stopped and most of the Polish troops got out.

It was clear the troops were experienced at what they were doing. The vehicles were properly spaced out (so that if one got hit with an improvised explosive device or direct Taliban attack, none of the other vehicles would be harmed). Some of the men dismounted to the right side of the unpaved road that wound through the village, orienting their automatic assault rifles to the right, and another group to the other side, guns poised for any threats that might arise from that side. Most of the armored trucks had a gunner mounted on top, with heavy machine guns, each pointed in different directions to ensure 360-degree coverage.

The farther we went into that first village, I saw more and more people warily watching us from their rooftops or walking nearby. About a third of the way in, we came by an area where maybe 20 men were sitting alongside the road watching silently as we went by, and on the roofs of a few homes was a group of women and children. All watched in silence. They didn't even appear to be talking among themselves. It was eerily quiet, with only the sounds of our vehicles' engines and marching boots of the soldiers as we traveled down the dirt road.

When we got beyond the edge of the village, the patrol leader motioned to his troops to take up a defensive position in which all the vehicles formed an oval and oriented weapon systems outwards so the unit leaders could meet safely in the middle to conduct a quick meeting. I talked with the lieutenant in charge of the patrol to better understand the purpose of these operations.

"How often do you patrol in this province, how often along this route, and what is the intended outcome?" I asked. He said they patrol periodically through the Ghazni countryside, maybe once every few weeks, and only go through the same villages once every six or eight weeks (there were scores of villages in their zone). The purpose, he told me, was to reassure the villagers of the presence of the International Security Assistance Force.

"When you come through villages like this one, do you stop at some point and conduct a meeting with the village elders?" I asked. "No," was his matter-of-fact reply. Perhaps it was clear on my face that I was perplexed because the Polish lieutenant laughed a bit and answered the question I was thinking: "Yes, we do nothing to limit the Taliban in this area. It takes us maybe 30 minutes to walk through this village, and then we're gone, not to return for maybe two months. It's little more than a nuisance for them."

Going Deeper in 2011

As bad as my initial impression had been in Ghazni, it was still just one province. It was entirely possible that once I started going to other parts of Afghanistan, I'd find a mixed bag: some areas were good, others marginal, and still others would be like Ghazni, where things were awful. Next up on my itinerary was the Kunar Province in eastern Afghanistan along the Afghan-Pakistani border.

In late January 2011, I was set to visit a unit from the famed 101st Airborne Division, the 1st Squadron, 32nd Cavalry out of Fort Campbell, Kentucky. While it was important on these site visits that I spent time with the regional commanders (two-star generals) and brigade commanders (full colonels), I always relished visiting the troopers at the company and platoon levels where the muddy boots on the ground did the hard work—and where truth couldn't be spun.

After my own direct combat experience in Desert Storm at the Battle of 73 Easting, I never lost the desire to engage the enemy at the point of the spear. These visits exposed something of a paradox in me. As I'll be the first to warn anyone, war is a horrible, brutish, destructive thing that is hellish both for those who conduct it and the civilian victims who suffer helplessly under it. Seriously, I hate war and do all I can to prevent it.

Yet there is also an indisputable allure to war for combat soldiers such as I that defies easy explanation. When I was with the 2nd U.S. Cavalry Regiment, poised to invade Iraq-held Kuwaiti territory in February 1991, I was eager to the point of suffering anxiety while awaiting the order to launch the attack. At the time, there was an 11th-hour attempt by Soviet Premier Mikhail Gorbachev to broker peace between then-President George H.W. Bush and Saddam Hussein. I and many of my cavalry mates were mortified, in real fear that at the very moment we were expecting to attack, the operation might be called off, forcing a return to our home base of Germany without having ever fought.

Here in Afghanistan, as a lieutenant colonel with no direct role in combat operations, I was nevertheless more than a little eager to perform my duties to assess conditions at the tip of the spear. As an avid student of military history, I was also excited about going into a combat zone alongside members of the 101st Airborne Division that had earned its reputation by parachuting into Normandy in 1944 and defeating the Nazis at the famed Battle of the Bulge. It didn't take long to discover that the troopers of 2011 were cut from the same stout cloth as their 1944 predecessors.

In fact, one of the things that so stood out to me in every single combat unit I visited (including the Polish brigade in Ghazni) was the high quality and professionalism of the troopers. They were, almost to a man, highly skilled, well-trained, disciplined, fearless, and dedicated to their mission. I also observed they largely cared for the Afghan people, often risked their own lives to defend the Afghan people, and were relentless in their attacks against the Taliban. Their attitude towards the Afghan military, however, was a different story.

When I met up with the 101st, the unit was in the process of shutting down some of the more isolated outposts in the Pech Valley of Kunar to reinforce higher priority, more populated locations. Their rationale made sense: we were producing nothing of any strategic value by occupying three large Forward Operating Bases in this hostile valley.

They planned to close three bases in the valley while holding onto the one at the mouth of the valley, ostensibly to deny giving the Taliban a free pass to other locations in Afghanistan. The Cav troopers were scheduled to go on a tactical patrol through the stunningly beautiful mountains of the Kunar River Valley and allowed me to accompany them.

The specific purpose of this mission was to visit the forward-most Afghan outpost in that part of Kunar Province where the Afghan police who manned the location had just been attacked by a Taliban patrol. The trip there was slow and treacherous, as we had to travel by heavily armored trucks along mountain roads that got increasingly narrow as we drove north along the Kunar River. At one point the truck I was driving in slipped slightly to the right, and we feared for a moment the vehicle might slide off the ledge and tumble into the river. When we got close to the outpost, we all dismounted and completed the journey on foot.

To consolidate bases, the unit needed to hand over some locations to Afghan-only control. The U.S. troops would be able to handle the plan with near-surgical precision, that much was clear, but the Americans were concerned about one aspect of the plan: Would the Afghan National Security Forces (ANSF) be able to hold when we left?

While on foot patrol in Kunar province

"Heck, no!" one cavalry officer told me as we approached the police base. "We really don't know what they'll do, but you and I both know they won't be able to handle that mission any time soon." If there was any doubt left in my mind, it was about to be dispelled.

When we arrived at the outpost, the 101st soldiers set up a hasty defensive perimeter around the police station and I accompanied our leader into a meeting with the chief of police. They exchanged pleasantries, shared tea as is the custom, and then began to discuss the attack that had happened earlier that day. As it turned out, it was a harassing attack in which Taliban fighters came in from the mountains overlooking the outpost and directed AK-47 automatic weapons' fire against the policemen. In this attack, no one had been killed, and the Taliban left.

When the meeting was near an end, I asked permission of my American patrol leader to ask some questions of the police chief. Through our interpreter, I said, "When you get attacks like this, what is your normal custom? Do you go after them? Do you periodically send harassing patrols of your own to try and disrupt the Taliban in your area?" The Afghan chief looked at the interpreter, and as he translated my question, I saw the chief's head whip around, look me directly in the face, and *laugh out loud*!

"No!" he said in an incredulous tone of voice, "that would be dangerous!" He viewed my question to be too absurd to even consider. Going out of his protected bunker after the men who attacked him? Ridiculous! They would not take actions they considered risky to themselves. And yet it should be an obvious, basic understanding to realize that if a group stays cloistered in a bunker and never goes out to meet the enemy, then the Taliban will be free to continue harassing fire, might kill some of the policemen, but more to the point, will have free reign throughout the area with no interference from the policemen.

In short, the purpose and intent of those policemen were not to protect the people living in the village adjacent to the outpost, but to protect themselves. The Taliban had nothing but contempt for the Afghan police and were not inhibited at all from operating in that area. Further, the American patrol leader told me that the U.S. only patrolled the area on occasion, and in any case, he said, "we only control about 100 meters on either side of this road—actually, make that *influence* 100 meters either side of the road—and the Taliban is totally free to do whatever they want everywhere else."

If the American public had known the truth of the situation in the Pech Valley in 2011, support for the war might have dried up and the people might have demanded their elected representatives end the pointless war. Instead, U.S. and NATO leaders spun the events and claimed successes that flatly didn't exist.

NATO spokesmen Gen. Joseph Blotz <u>told The Washington Post</u> in late February 2011 that the "Afghan security forces are able to take responsibility of the Pech Valley." This transition demonstrated, "is testimony to our confidence" in the Afghan military. That optimistic view was complete fiction, as I had personally observed, but even Afghan military leaders disputed the ISAF spokesman.

A battalion executive officer of one of the ANSF units in that area, however, had a rather different view. It would be "a suicide mission" to hand tactical control to Afghan units in the area, Afghan Major Traub (who only uses one name) <u>told The New York Times</u>. Based on his experience operating in the Pech Valley area, Major Taub added that "it's absolutely impractical for the Afghan National Army to protect the area without the Americans." His words—ignored by U.S. and NATO leaders—were to prove prophetic just months later.

Just several months later the Afghan forces proved incapable of providing security against the insurgents in the Pech—just as Major Truab had predicted—and U.S. leaders decided to send American forces right back into the Pech Valley. But instead of simply admitting we were wrong in believing the Afghan military could handle the security without American troops, U.S. officials vigorously denied there had been any trouble and that the reason our troops had been sent back had nothing to do with the inability of the Afghan troops to hold the valley.

An Associated Press article in mid-August <u>reported that</u> "[j]ust months after pulling out of a remote slice of eastern Afghanistan dubbed the 'Valley of Death,' U.S. troops are back reinforcing their once-abandoned bases in the area—a hotbed of the insurgency and a dangerous second front in the decade-old war."

The official U.S spokesman claimed the move to put American troops back in the Pech wasn't due to enemy advance or ANSF incapacity, <u>but merely</u> "a matter of where [American troops] laid their heads at night" – which every Western troop who had served on the ground in Afghanistan knew was untrue.

It is instructive to examine what the U.S. gained by sending our troops back into the Pech in August 2011.

After Obama's December 2009 order to deploy the surge in Afghanistan, the majority of the American combat units withdrew in 2014. What happened to the Pech?

Absent the American troops there, and with the Taliban maintaining their presence, one might think that today the population there is under the tyranny of the Taliban. On the contrary, in a 2016 report, Radio Free Europe/Radio Liberty interviewed some of the Pech residents who had lived there since before the surge. A dramatically different picture emerged.

Two years after the NATO withdrawal from the Pech Valley, the radio reported, "A tentative peace has returned to the region. Violence levels have dropped significantly, and attacks on the Afghan security forces are rare."

One resident, Zabihullah (who used only one name), added hopefully, "We are now hoping this region will soon be called the 'valley of peace.'"

How did this remarkable transformation to relative peace occur?

According to another resident, Zaiur Rahman, the absence of Western counterterror forces was a major contributing factor. "When the foreign forces were here," Rahman said, "our roads were sometimes closed for hours… There was no security, and attacks, bomb blasts, and airstrikes were common." But violence dramatically decreased when the Western troops left and the city elders took the matter to the Taliban to resolve their disputes using centuries-old Afghan methods.

Rahman said the local religious leaders "made it clear that fighting against the Afghan security forces was not justifiable and would be treated as aggression and cruelty" under interpretations of genuine Sharia law. In 2019, Radio Free Afghanistan reported that the peace has held and now there is virtually no fighting. It is no coincidence that before the arrival of U.S. troops in the Pech there was no fighting – and after they left, the fighting ended.

I left the 101st Airborne troops in the Pech at the end of January 2011, discouraged at the gulf I had observed between what our leaders claimed and what I observed on the ground. This trip would prove to be only the first of many such realizations.

In the next few months, I visited units in Khost, Paktika, Kunduz, Balkh, Nangarhar, and Kandahar provinces and saw the same negative fundamentals generally at play. The more I traveled, the more I came to realize the rosy picture being painted back home was not merely inaccurate, but closer to sheer fantasy. In March 2011, my emotions started to change from discouragement to outright anger.

101ˢᵗ Airborne soldiers on a break during a patrol near the Kunar River

On March 15, Petraeus again went to Congress with Undersecretary Flournoy to report on progress in Afghanistan. In the previous summer's testimony, Petraeus had said the coalition was enjoying "early success" as they got "the inputs right." In March, he confidently asserted that the U.S. coalition had made clear progress.

"As a bottom line up front," the general told Sen. John McCain, chairman of the Senate Armed Services Committee, "it is ISAF's assessment that the momentum achieved by the Taliban in Afghanistan since 2005 has been arrested in much of the country and reversed in a number of important areas." Yes, he admitted, the gains were "fragile and reversible," but unequivocally communicated to the members that things were moving in the right direction.

He warned Congress not to waver in its commitment and continue to back the plan. "Although the insurgents are already striving to regain lost momentum and lost safe havens as we enter the spring fighting season," Petraeus said, the U.S. would only be able to "build on the momentum achieved in 2010" through "additional tough fighting." His direct implication—that the surge was working and would only succeed if we pressed on with the fighting—angered me greatly.

Because of what I had already seen in the previous four months I *knew* that the claims of improvement were illusory. I knew that if the American people and Congress realized the truth of things, that after more than a year of giving the new surge a chance that things were getting *worse*, then they would likely demand the mission either dramatically change to something that had a chance of success or that it be ended outright.

But there was no contrasting voice to Petraeus' cheery version of events. Left unchallenged, he succeeded in portraying success to the American people, including the president. Three weeks after his testimony, rumors began to swirl around Washington that Obama was going to reward Petraeus with a promotion for his success in Afghanistan: elevation to become the Director of the CIA.

Before the end of April, the rumors were confirmed and Petraeus' nomination was made public. Though few knew it at the time, the war was deteriorating quickly as Petraeus' fame and reputation were skyrocketing – and the stark incongruity likewise caused my anger to rise. Unfortunately, there were more ugly truths awaiting my discovery that would soon push my anger beyond the boiling point.

The Zharay Assessment

In June 2011, I went to Kandahar Province for the first time, visiting units from a brigade of the 10th Mountain Division. First, I met with the brigade staff at FOB Pasab to get the view from the top, then met with the battalion commander and staff at Combat Outpost Howz-e Madad. After hearing the leaders' thoughts at the two headquarters, I finally went to Combat Outpost Nalgham in Kandahar Province's Zharay District, meeting with the company commander and line troops. This is where the rubber meets the road: company and platoon-level are where the combat takes place and where ground-truth is most readily found.

The day after I arrived at Nalgham, I accompanied a platoon from Combat Company, 1-32 Infantry, on a patrol to a building complex that had just been the scene of fierce fighting and cleared of Taliban fighters the night before. The patrol's assignment was a joint force mission composed of one U.S. platoon and an Afghan National Army squad to establish a strong defensive position against the Taliban at the building complex.

The mission was designed to push the Taliban farther out of the area. The units' tasks were to clear the complex of any booby traps that may have been left behind by the Taliban and then establish machine gun positions and observations posts from rooftops. What I observed, however, was the polar opposite of what was supposed to happen.

No one expects the Afghan army to perform anywhere near the level of a well-trained U.S. force, but they are expected to put forth the effort and show genuine effort and a willingness to learn. But it was evident to me from the beginning of the mission that the U.S. troopers had utter contempt for the ANA. It didn't take me long to figure out why.

The complex was still seeded with an unknown number of IEDs when we arrived, and intelligence told us the Taliban were likely hiding in some buildings about 200 yards across a grape field from our forward-most fighting position. The temperature that day was a suffocating 116 degrees. As with other patrols in which I participated, we drove part of the way there in our armored combat vehicles and then dismounted to go the rest of the way on foot.

My gear was typical for an American trooper on patrol: an M4 carbine, a 9 mm pistol, Kevlar helmet, Kevlar body armor, extra ammunition, water, and other necessary gear, which all together weighed about 80 pounds. Carry that much gear in 116-degree heat and it doesn't take long to become exhausted.

Upon arrival at the objective, the American troops did exactly what they were supposed to do: heat or no heat, they immediately went to work clearing the area of IEDs, building machine gun positions, and preparing defensive works throughout the complex.

The U.S. troops were professional, focused, and relentless. They did what the combat situation required, meaning the mission came first and personal needs second; four of the soldiers suffered minor heat injuries and needed to be cooled down with water after the work had been done.

The ANA troops, however, had no intention of working hard. Instead of clearing the buildings for enemy traps or building defensive positions, they quite literally went directly to the shade in one of the bombed-out rooms and immediately took naps; they made no effort to complete a single task.

The whole time I was there, they did nothing to help the U.S. troops and showed no interest in making the area secure, being instead content to allow the Americans to do all the work. It's not hard to understand why the American soldiers would have had contempt for the ANA men.

U.S. infantrymen were there in hostile territory, under grueling conditions, and just the previous day five Americans had been wounded in action against the Taliban. Our soldiers were there to help the Afghan people defeat the Taliban and make the country secure.

Yet while our troops struggled and sacrificed for the benefit of the Afghan people, their troops seemed unconcerned and demonstrated little interest in learning how to become an effective, professional fighting force. If the observations made in Pech and Zharay were isolated or were balanced out by other impressive examples, it might not have been so bad. As the summer wore on, however, I discovered very few positive stories to relate.

After I had made three more months' worth of unit visits and combat patrols, Petraeus was installed as the CIA Director, and Marine 4-star Gen. John Allen took his place as the new commander. By mid-June, I began to wonder if Obama would stick to his original plan to start withdrawing the surge troops in July, or whether General Allen would ignore the deadline and make a request for more time.

In his famous "New way forward" speech at West Point in December 2009, Obama had declared that after "18 months, our troops will begin to come home." The operation started in January 2010, meaning sometime in July 2011 the surge troops were scheduled to withdraw.

Even without stepping one foot on the ground in Afghanistan, I realized there was little chance we could turn around a war that was allegedly on the brink of failure in such a short time. Once I got to Afghanistan, however, I realized it wasn't little chance: it was zero.

What would happen, I wondered, if we stuck to the plan and began withdrawing troops in the absence of success? Nothing good, obviously.

But in Obama's defense, as far as he was being told by his senior generals, the plan *was* succeeding.

At the time, Petraeus and his many defenders in the media lauded the general for reprising a presumed surge victory in 2007 Iraq. Years after the <u>failure was exposed</u>, however, the hawks in Washington had to find someone besides Petraeus to scapegoat. The chosen victim: Obama.

In the years since the surge ended, some counterinsurgency apologists have argued that Petraeus' strategy in Afghanistan was solid but ultimately failed because Obama didn't give him enough troops, and in any case, setting "<u>an arbitrary withdrawal date</u>" of July 2011 was Obama's greatest mistake. Yet even today few realize the mistake wasn't so much Obama's as it was that of Petraeus and Admiral Mike Mullen, chairman of the Joint Chiefs of Staff in 2009.

Before Obama announced the new Afghan surge, he had conducted months of assessments in the West Wing. In the final analysis, and before he made the final call, Obama called his most senior advisors into the Oval Office, among whom were Mullen, Petraeus, Secretary of State Hillary Clinton, and Secretary of Defense Robert Gates. In a detailed rendering of that fateful meeting, author Jonathan Alter published a 2010 article in <u>Newsweek</u> that revealed how the military ultimately succeeded in persuading the president to order the surge.

Obama had insisted, Alter wrote, that the mission not be an open-ended counterinsurgency operation, but one based on protecting major population centers while training Afghan forces within an 18-month window. If the military couldn't execute the mission in that timeframe, the president would likely not authorize the deployment. <u>Alter revealed</u> the key moment when the military leaders convinced Obama they could do it:

> *Inside the Oval Office, Obama asked Petraeus, "David, tell me now. I want you to be honest with me. You can do this in 18 months?"*
>
> *"Sir, I'm confident we can train and hand over to the ANA [Afghan National Army] in that time frame," Petraeus replied.*

"Good. No problem," the president said. "If you can't do the things you say you can in 18 months, then no one is going to suggest we stay, right?"

"Yes, sir, in agreement," Petraeus said.

"Yes, sir," Mullen said.

The president was crisp but informal. "Bob, you have any problems?" he asked Gates, who said he was fine with it.

The president then encapsulated the new policy: in quickly, out quickly, focus on Al Qaeda, and build the Afghan Army. "I'm not asking you to change what you believe, but if you don't agree with me that we can execute this, say so now," he said. No one said anything.

"Tell me now," Obama repeated.

"Fully support, sir," Mullen said.

"Ditto," Petraeus said.

Whether the three Pentagon leaders believed they could accomplish the mission in 18 months or whether they believed that when the time came, they could convince the young president to extend the deadline, isn't certain.

What *is* certain, however, is that both the strategy they used and the timeframe they agreed upon utterly condemned the mission to failure. Obama was the president and is ultimately responsible for the results of his decisions. But the far, far greater failure lies with the military leaders who sold Obama on an unwinnable strategy.

Yet in late June 2011, few in America, including the president, realized that we were losing the war. Because of the public statements by Petraeus and other senior leaders saying we were winning, Obama announced on June 23 that his promised withdrawal was going to begin, on schedule, the next month.

Obama told the nation we were winning the war and "achieving our goals," and would begin the drawdown from "a position of strength."

He ordered that the 33,000 surge troops he had authorized in December 2009 would begin methodically returning home, with 10,000 leaving by the end of 2011 and the remaining 23,000 by September of the following year. Based on what I already knew, this decision would have disastrous, predictable consequences.

On July 8, 2011, I made an entry in my journal describing my thoughts at that time. It would begin a process that would eventually lead me, in February 2012, to go public with the truth and expose that our senior leaders had known, at the time, the war was being lost—yet willfully deceived the government and public into believing the opposite. From my headquarters at Bagram Air Base, I wrote:

If we continue to go forward as things sit right now, we will likely fail. The mission will degenerate, and when we get to next summer and it is clear that the ANSF aren't close to being ready to take over their security; the corruption of the government will continue unabated and, in some cases, will actually degenerate. The powerbrokers and warlordism will rise again to the fore, fragmenting what little authority exists in Kabul, as every level of government proves incapable of providing basic services. Pakistan will deepen its intelligence service's hold on all elements of the insurgency.

Then, regrettably, last and least, is the people of Afghanistan. They will not be fooled in the least by the rhetoric of victory ISAF will continue to publicly proclaim, they will have even less reason to support GoIRA (the Government of the Islamic Republic of Afghanistan, the official title of the Afghan government) at the expense of crossing either the Taliban, the warlords, or the local and regional powerbrokers—and they certainly won't side with the United States, as despite what every American uniformed leader wishes they would think, they know—correctly—that the exodus has begun and that we are going to leave.

The people will remain the poorest on the planet, ruled by the most corrupt governing system on earth. The regional stakeholders will revert to low-level proxy involvement; even through all this devolution, the West will remain in some token level, probably in Kabul, Bagram, and Kandahar, ensuring none of the regional countries get too forceful in their interest of things inside Afghanistan, thus guaranteeing the internationally recognized borders of Afghanistan will remain "inviolable" and intact, thus preserving the appearance, no matter how transparently foolish, that we did not "abandon" them this time.

Before I decided to take public action, however, I thought I would take the comparatively lower risk of trying to reengage with Jay Carney, now elevated to the position of White House press secretary, and Tony Blinken, the vice president's national security advisor. I was fairly certain the only information the president had been given was the rosy picture painted by Petraeus and others, so I decided to reach out to Jay and Tony to give them the genuine on-the-ground view.

I sent my first note on July 12, 2011, which read in part:

In the paragraphs that follow, I will lay out what my observations, experience, and research suggest how the end game will play out here in Afghanistan in response to the president's announced drawdown schedule and how it is being implemented by the senior ISAF leaders.

Bottom line up front*: I assess our current chances for an acceptable political or military outcome for the United States by 2014 to be less than 20 percent.*

Based on the above assumptions, and beginning with conditions as they exist on July 12, 2011, I project the following are likely to occur or exist between now and December 2013:

- *The ANSF is not and will not be able to effectively handle security in insurgent-contested zones even by 2014; most independent observers accept this as a given.*

- *As it becomes evident the ANSF cannot mount an effective defense against the Taliban (TB), the Afghan government at every echelon will increase and accelerate their level of corruption; they will make private, individual deals with the TB and they will horde money to ensure their survival during and after the end-game.*

- *Powerbrokers and warlordism will rise again, supported by militia forces that are already spreading around the country, fragmenting further GoIRA's authority.*

- *Pakistan covertly deepens its ISI-hold on many elements of the insurgency (INS) while continuing publicly to strive with both Karzai and the US to find a solution to a deteriorating situation.*

- *Iran, Russia, Turkmenistan, Uzbekistan, Tajikistan, Kazakhstan, and China all put considerably more effort in ensuring their individual national interests are safeguarded, without consideration of how their actions might affect the U.S.*

- *India will not sit idly by and watch Pakistan increase its influence in AFG, and will also engage their own proxies to limit Pakistani benefit.*

- *The people of Afghanistan will not be fooled (and are not currently fooled) by the continued ISAF victory narrative. As time passes, the people will have less and less incentive to support GoIRA by risking the ire of the Taliban, the warlords, or the local and regional powerbrokers.*

- *As the density of ISAF troops continues to fall, some of the INS groups will begin to fragment, just as they did in the post-Soviet days, and numerous local and regional blocs will form, tied in one way or another to tribe, clan and village.*

- *Even as some INS groups begin to fight each other, the leaders of the key groups will become less willing to give in on negotiations, as their force ratio vis-à-vis the ISAF/ANSF military forces improves with each series of redeployments;*

- *If ISAF follows through on its claim of shifting the focus of the fighting from the south to the east, we can expect that in every place an American boot is removed and transferred to RC-East, a Taliban sandal will replace it; the ANSF— even in the south—is years away from basic independent capability and will not be able to resist TB return.*

- *Between now and the end of 2014, upwards of another 1,000 American Service members will be killed in action, ~5,000 more wounded (a thousand of which will suffer amputations of one or more limbs), and thousands more ANSF members and AFG civilians will be killed. These all will have been killed and wounded for no additional security or political gain for the United States.*

As he was throughout, Carney was kind and respectful and did not ridicule me for reaching out to him. I knew there was only a sliver of a chance he would take this to the president and even less that Obama would make a radical change in policy this late in the game. But I was desperate. Even a sliver of hope is better than the absolute zero that was assured by doing nothing.

The next month I sent Carney another note, this time with an alternative policy Obama could consider. My thoughts were that if through his own intelligence sources he began to realize that his senior leaders were deceiving him and he realized his plan would fail, perhaps the president would consider a different approach that might have a chance. I wrote:

I am presently in Khost Province. What I've seen here is typical of what I'm told is going on all over Afghanistan. Everyone here knows the end game has begun – the Afghan government, U.S. and NATO troops, the Taliban and the Afghan people. Instead of bleeding hundreds of billions more US dollars and thousands more lives (on all sides), we could move to the endgame now.

It was always without evidence that some of our senior defense officials suggested the Taliban would not negotiate until they had "realized they could not win on the battlefield." The Taliban have always known they couldn't defeat us on the battlefield (but they are more than willing to negotiate). Rather than slug out another three or so years of combat that will accomplish nothing, we could work with numerous key leaders to announce a cease-fire while we negotiate an end to hostilities.

It is in everyone's benefit (ours, our NATO allies, GoIRA, the TB and the AFG people), and with determination and a skillful hand at the helm a ceasefire could be done, I am convinced, in between three to six months.

I am convinced the President is uniquely capable of making this happen, as his reputation for bringing 'change' and his Nobel Peace Prize credentials can't be matched.

This would be very difficult—even agonizing at times—but it is definitely doable because the main players in Afghanistan are culturally predisposed to arriving at such a conclusion, and after a decade of war, all parties are ready to wrap this up and start focusing on other, legitimately pressing needs.

Let me know if there is further interest.

There was no further interest, of course, but again Jay was professional and respectful in his dealings with me, never ridiculing my efforts.

One week later I was visiting another unit in the Khost province, 6th Squadron, 4th Cavalry. As with every other visit, I was vastly impressed with the quality of the U.S. soldiers and their commitment to duty. But this visit was a little different than most others.

I had already been struggling emotionally because just days before the visit, on Aug. 15, I had gone to the mess hall at Bagram Air Base where my main headquarters was located, and seen a copy of the Stars and Stripes on the newsstand and noticed the huge headline: "My whole squad is gone" and a picture of a mangled combat vehicle beneath it.

Front page of Stars & Stripes newspaper that gave me the bad news about the troopers I had met.

As it turned out, I had met two of the men killed in the blast. Their boss, an Army staff sergeant, had bragged about two men, Specialist Jameel T. Freeman and Specialist Jordan M. Morris, as we rested during a patrol on a stiflingly hot day. They were hard workers, never complained, and had overcome some major hardships in life. To this day, I can still picture them working across the courtyard of a bombed-out building we were using as a temporary patrol base; two young men whose tough Army boss was beaming with pride as he described them. They had such bright futures... until an IED ended everything for them and their families.

As I got to the cavalry unit's location in Khost, I discovered that they had just lost their first sergeant in an IED blast, and several other troopers were seriously wounded. I recorded some of the more disheartening discoveries in my journal during my stay there—and my anger rose to yet another level of intensity. On Aug. 19, I wrote:

> *I realize this is becoming an all too familiar entry, but I am growing in anger, seething at the absurdity and unconcern for the life of my fellow Soldiers displayed by so many in ranks at Brigade and above in this theater.*

> *But at the company level, it's almost uniformly the same. Regardless of which part of Afghanistan I go to, the Soldiers at the company, platoon, squad, and individual level almost all tell me the same thing: this mission is absurd, it can't be accomplished with the resources we've placed against it, our men are dying and having their limbs blown off every day, the various stripes of the ANSF are almost entirely*

incapable – and display very little interest in trying to become so.

*I heard again here from the company commander [*Editor's note: we will refer to him as "Captain Allen" because Davis was unable to contact the captain to request permission to use his real name*]: Some of the ANSF have been heard on intercepted radio calls making deals with the local Taliban, and thus have almost no motivation to aggressively get after them.*

In Capt. Allen's battle zone, he is restricted to two main roads, and has to patrol very frequently to keep them open. He has well over 40 square kilometers of battlespace he's responsible for but can't get off the roads anywhere or he risks getting his men blown up. He repeated something to me I've heard several other leaders on previous patrols: "How do I look these men in the eye and ask them to go out day after day on these missions? What's even harder: how do I look my First Sergeant's wife in the eye when I get back and tell her that her husband died for something meaningful? How do I do that?"

This is really starting to get old. If I could go some places in the tactical fight and find a few locations where things were going well, I might be able to generate some optimism.

But there are none.

*My friend, there are none. Instead, I keep seeing instances like the one in which a brigade executive officer told me with a straight face that the ANA [*Afghan National Army*] is doing "well" while the Afghan National Police just "needed a little help," but overall definite progress was being made. Yet when I go from their headquarters down to view things from the ground with the men who've lived it every day, I see physical evidence of the opposite.*

And what remains consistent that drives me absolutely nuts (really, it's increasing my anger) is that the cost of this fiction is the lives of the men who live day after day in the battlespace, men like those five men of Charlie Company who were killed last week in an IED blast, like the First Sergeant of this unit who was "blown into five pieces" one month ago (July 17, I believe they said)—or those who may die tomorrow, or surely will die between now and the next eight months among the men of CPT Allen's company.

Maybe it'll even be me. Perhaps during tomorrow's patrol it'll be my turn. Because I know that's possible, I made a last video statement to my little sons and sent it to my brother-in-law. I asked him to keep the video and share it with my sons when they are old enough to understand, telling them how deeply I loved them; specifying to each individually how much I loved them, what about them I love so much, and finally that my unequivocal main hope in life is that they find a personal relationship with Jesus Christ—and that between now and the time they come home I'll ask Jesus if He would be so kind as to reserve a mansion near mine for my sons!

Anyway, at least in death there will be the first and foremost brilliant and wonderful privilege and unequaled joy of seeing Jesus face-to-face, and then the hope of seeing my sons again in a beautiful place with no tears or sin.

Gosh, that sounds like a real nice place to be right about now…

Nearing the Ending of my Deployment—and the Beginning of My Decision to Go Public

During my first taste of combat, I was a green 2nd lieutenant fighting with the 2nd U.S. Cavalry in Desert Storm. Our unit fought in the largest tank battle since World War II at the Battle of 73 Easting. We fought a brigade of the Iraqi Republican Guards in an hours-long engagement that included tank-on-tank fire, armored infantry vehicles firing wire-guided missiles, mortar fire, machine guns, artillery rounds, and short-range rockets flying all over the battlefield.

During my 2005 combat tour to Afghanistan, I never saw a bullet fired in anger. I spent most of my time in a headquarters building as a liaison officer between Central Command and my Combined Forces Command, Afghanistan HQ in Tampa and Qatar, and some time in Kabul. My 2009 combat tour to Iraq was cut short because of medical problems, but in the 5,000 or so miles I traveled in the border region of Mason Province, I never fired a weapon or experienced hostile fire.

During this deployment, however, there were several times I was with U.S. troops who were fired on by hostile Taliban fighters. One of the more poignant came on the 10th anniversary of the 9/11 terrorist attacks that spawned our mission in the first place. I recorded the surreal event in my journal the next day when I returned to my headquarters in Bagram.

September 12, 2011

So very much has happened since my last entry, but I'm just flat too tired right now to record any details. I've been rocketed multiple times at Bagram (have never been hit, of course), had a mortar fall within 75 meters of my position at FOB [forward operating base] Wright near Asadabad, Afghanistan, and endured two Taliban attacks against COP [combat outpost] Monti, one of which began with a mortar and machinegun attack while I and two others were on the landing zone waiting to leave as the helicopter in sight and began its descent – and this happened on the 10th anniversary of 9/11.

Somehow it seemed appropriate on that 10th anniversary to run an American flag up the pole at the headquarters of Bravo Company, 2-27 Infantry Regiment at COP Monti (astride the city of Asmar, Afghanistan) on the morning of September 11, 2011.

I was only about six weeks away from the end of my combat deployment. Soon I would have to make the final decision about whether I would take the enormous risk of going public with my assertion that our leaders were deceiving the public about the war, or if I would conclude that it would be pointless and result in zero change, and simply keep my mouth shut and my career preserved.

Lt. Col. Davis, in the Kunar River Valley, eastern Afghanistan, 2011

In addition to the attacks made against my position mentioned in my journal entry, I had also stepped on an IED while on a patrol in the Argandab River Valley in Kandahar Province – which miraculously did not explode. I was also nearly blown up by a Taliban rocket attack while simply walking across the compound of an obscure base in eastern Afghanistan on my way to the chow hall. After the attack, I had to just shake my head and be thankful the rocket impacted far enough away from me that I wasn't hurt—it would have been quite un-heroic for my family to have been told I had been killed in action *while going to lunch*!.

But weighing more heavily on my mind than my own brushes with death were the <u>more than 400 Americans</u> who had been killed and <u>more than 5,000</u> who had been wounded since my arrival in Afghanistan. Absolutely oppressive on my spirit were the ones yet to die if we just blindly continued this mission without change.

If I came forward and publicly revealed what I experienced and knew of the truth behind the falsely optimistic picture painted by some of our highest-ranking leaders, most likely too few in the public would believe me over the generals and I'd be buried in obscurity (or worse: I'd be crushed by the government as other whistleblowers before me had been).

What sense would it make, then, to potentially lose my career and find myself in serious hardship if the chances of success were so minuscule? While weighing the pros and cons, I decided to build a case during the final few weeks of my deployment and document the circumstances of my claims.

After I got back to the U.S., I decided, I would seek the counsel and advice of a few close friends I trusted and make the final call. When I compiled all my experiences and calculated the distance I had traveled throughout the country, I was surprised by what I found. While waiting in the tactical passenger terminal at Bagram Airfield to leave the country, I made one last journal entry:

October 26, 2011

Well, I had time for one more entry (I'm in the holding area at the Bagram air terminal awaiting my C17 flight to Kuwait).

As it turned out, I travelled over 9,000 miles throughout the course of my deployment, and even I was surprised at the number of places I'd visited and things I'd done. When you add in the over 250 Soldier interviews I conducted and the literally thousands of pages of intelligence I read, I really do have a pretty good comprehensive understanding of this war in its current state.

One thing I fully validated during my deployment is that since 2004 general officers have been claiming success in every metric of alleged success, yet the most crucial indices unequivocally demonstrate unchanged deterioration in the war, not the "progress" they so often cited. My observations over the past year have confirmed the following:

1) The ANSF are not capable, have not been capable, and are only now marginally better (in some categories) than in the past. No evidence whatsoever exists that indicates they will be in even marginally better shape when this mission is set to end in 2014.

2) The GoIRA is as corrupt, almost without qualification, as it was in 2005.

3) The people are no closer to supporting the government and opposing the insurgency than they were in 2005, and some evidence suggests they are actually slightly more supportive of the Taliban than they have been since the war began.

4). All key stats show unambiguously how the number of violent attacks by the Taliban have risen in concert with the number of U.S./NATO troops deployed. While overall violence this month may be down, IEDs are up, and violence in RC (Regional Command) Southwest and East is above even 2010 levels.

5). Lastly, U.S. casualty rates are dramatically higher as a result of the surge—and remain on a continuing and rising arc as they have since 2005.

In addition to those specific metrics, other fundamentals of war also argued persuasively that our military mission had been failing since at least 2005 and would continue to fail in the future unless major changes were made. One of <u>McChrystal's</u> and later Petraeus' most frequently cited requirements for winning counterinsurgency battles was to live among the people. "The people are the center of gravity," Petraeus <u>told the troops</u> fighting in Afghanistan in 2010.

"Take off your sunglasses," when going on patrols in Afghan villages, the general had told the troops. "Situational awareness can only be gained by interacting face to face, not separated by ballistic glass or Oakleys." But in practice, that engagement rarely happened—and even when it did, the effect was more often than not to create fear in the villagers, not reassure them.

Throughout the many patrols I conducted with American units during my year there, I would typically see a U.S. combat unit conduct a "presence patrol" as they're called, by driving or walking through a village. Sometimes it was like that December 2010 Polish patrol where we didn't talk to anyone, didn't ask questions, and didn't appear interested in listening to anything they might want to tell us.

Other times we briefly engaged with village elders, but in *all* cases, the patrol lasted a mere moment and then we were gone. As we say in the Army, Petraeus' ideas "brief well" on paper or to an audience that doesn't have direct experience, but on the dirty ground where reality lives, believing that we would succeed by periodically visiting people was a futile exercise in self-delusion.

The Taliban, in contrast, quite often lived *among* the people, or at least was a permanent and routine presence. Logically, it would be foolish for the population to side with us because we could offer only token, periodic presence among some of the villages, while in other, whole sections of provinces, we never stepped foot. The Taliban was infamous for intimidating, threatening, or killing locals <u>who worked with us</u>, while we could do almost nothing to protect them.

Because the ANSF was woefully inadequate (and in any event rarely ventured out of their static checkpoints or isolated bases), there was no one to protect the population from the Taliban. This was reinforced in *every single location* I visited in 2010-11 that our military presence in Afghanistan was a charade; it had no genuine military purpose and could never, regardless of how many years we stayed, how many troops we deployed, or how hard we tried, produce a military victory.

With our highly trained troops, state-of-the-art equipment, advanced technology, and a limitless logistics system, we could impose our tactical will on Taliban fighters in 100 percent of direct-fire engagements. No matter how valiantly the Taliban tried to fight, as I saw firsthand, it was suicide for them to attempt to engage us directly.

That's why they rarely tried.

But tactically defeating the superior U.S. military was never their objective. Instead, they would conduct harassing operations, plant thousands of IEDs along the many roads, and conduct <u>assassination operations</u> against key Afghan leaders—all to make continuing the war so costly and loathsome to us, that eventually we would tire and leave the field of battle.

ISAF forces would try to defeat the Taliban by conducting intelligence-driven <u>night raids</u> and other tactical operations when we could find large numbers of them at a training facility, but it was akin to trying to drain Lake Michigan with an eyedropper.

Yes, you could succeed in every Special Operations mission and successfully take out key enemy leaders with precision drone strikes, but it would never make any difference. As soon as one leader was killed, one or two took his place almost immediately—and that has been the case since the insurgency started to emerge in 2003.

When I was first assigned to Afghanistan in 2005, I was told the Taliban was estimated to include between 1,500 and 2,000 members. During my 2010-11 deployment, it was reportedly between 10,000 and 20,000. Yet by 2018, an Afghan general claimed there was a <u>staggering 77,000 Taliban</u>.

We are reported to have killed tens of thousands of Taliban fighters since the war began, but 15 years and two surges after I was first deployed there, the number of Taliban has *increased* by upwards of 70,000, and as of this writing (early 2020), they <u>control or contest</u> more Afghan territory than at any time since 2001.

By every metric that matters, it is painfully clear now—and should have been clear long ago—that the war in Afghanistan was unwinnable. Nothing changed from the time I was there in 2005, throughout 2011, and continues to be the case today: *we will never win a military victory.*

The perpetual support for sending regular rotations of American troops to Afghanistan—many of whom will needlessly die or lose limbs—while spending scores of billions a year should be repulsive to every American. It was repulsive to me as I landed in Washington, D.C. that October.

Even before my plane finished taxiing down the runway at Reagan National Airport that rainy day, I knew the die was already cast: I *had* to go public; I didn't need to confer with anyone.

I was convicted in my spirit and soul that knowing the war was being lost, knowing that men would continue to die pointless combat deaths, knowing our leaders were lying to the American public, and yet remaining silent because it would cost me personally would be moral cowardness.

I didn't want to be a martyr, and I definitely did not want to find myself the target of the Pentagon's senior leaders' ire, but in the end, I was *unable* to remain silent. If I kept my mouth shut to protect myself and the expected happened – the loss of hundreds of more lives and tens of thousands more wounded – I would feel like a coward, haunted for the rest of my life for failing to at least try to help them.

Going Public

After my return to the U.S., I was still a part of the Fort Belvoir-based Rapid Equipping Force and was assigned duty as the liaison officer between the REF and the Army's senior generals in the Pentagon. Ordinarily, it would be a plum position, especially working with senior leadership. I had served in the Army Operation Center at the Pentagon from 2002 until my deployment to Afghanistan in 2005 and loved it. What was to come would be about as far from love as one could get.

In the first few weeks after my return, I was advised by several veterans, experts in whistleblowing, and others who had themselves blown the whistle on government fraud, waste, or abuse. They included Matthew Hoh, a former Marine officer and former State Department official, and Danielle Brian, director of the Program on Government Oversight.

Matt had fought in the worst of the Iraq war in 2007 as an engineer company commander and had taken one of the most courageous stands of any high-ranking State Department official. In 2009, he made front-page news by resigning his post in Afghanistan to protest President Obama's surge strategy, which Matt knew would fail. Danielle — known as the "dean of the watchdogs" — had long been a champion of those without power; she inspired me to remain true to my convictions. Both Matt and Danielle have remained close friends.

Some veterans had tried to dissuade me from going public, saying it wouldn't make any difference and would just harm me. But all of them helped prepare me emotionally for what was to come and were an enormous source of encouragement and support once I made clear I was committed to going public.

One of the veterans of our group had arranged an introduction with a writer from The New York Times, Scott Shane. We met several times during a few weeks; eventually, he agreed to write a story on my public claims. I told him I had compiled a classified document detailing specific, secret details that graphically illustrated the gap between what public leaders said in public and what they knew in private.

I had no intention, though, of becoming the next Bradley Manning, the Army enlisted soldier who had <u>illegally released</u> thousands of classified files to Wikileaks. I would reveal nothing about that report, and would instead be giving it to select members of the House of Representatives and Senate.

But I did plan on writing an explosive article of my own in the Armed Forces Journal, where I had been published several times in years past. Eventually, Shane got together with the editor of the AFJ at the time, Bradley Peniston (<u>currently deputy editor</u> of Defense One), and in mid-January the two of them selected a date to simultaneously publish my story.

The New York Times wanted to be the exclusive outlet to publish the shocking news that an active-duty Army officer was going public with criticism of the war, and the AFJ would have the exclusive rights to publish my actual criticisms. The date chosen was Feb. 5, 2012.

I was glad on the one hand that we now had a fixed date—but it started a continual rise in stress and pressure. I couldn't afford to let this news catch my Army bosses in stunned surprise; I would have to face the music and tell them face-to-face. I won't lie: the stress began to consume me as the day drew near when I had to come clean.

Before I revealed myself, however, I sought a measure of potential security. When I had published a critical analysis of the Army's premier modernization system, the Future Combat Systems, in a 2008 edition of the Armed Forces Journal, I did not take the precaution of lining up support from anyone outside the Army.

That my work was the <u>featured cover story</u> concluding that the Army brass needed to make major changes in their favorite program didn't make me any friends at the top. I was made to pay a severe personal price by the Army leadership at that time; no one had had my back at that time. I didn't want to make that mistake again.

So, before publication or telling anyone in the Army, my informal advisory group arranged for me to meet with several members of the U.S. House and four members of the Senate to tell my story. The three members of Congress who were most supportive were Republican Walter Jones of North Carolina, Democrat Jim McGovern of Massachusetts, and Democrat

Davis meeting with Rep. Walter Jones in his Washington, DC office, early 2012

Barbara Lee of California. Each of those House members, along with one prominent senator, told me that if the Army leadership took any action against me after I went public that I was to let them know immediately and they would help me.

I intended to do the right thing no matter the consequences, but that didn't mean I would be careless and defenseless. I thought having all these members on my side *before* I revealed anything to Army leadership just might keep them from taking any permanently damaging action against me.

Just three days after The New York Times published its story, on Feb. 8, Representative McGovern went to the House floor and made an impassioned defense of my report and specifically mentioned that we had spoken. That speech and the backing of the other members of Congress probably helped temper any desire Army leadership might have had in trying to inflict retribution against me.

But none of that was going to help me when I had to disclose to my bosses one-on-one what I had done. I knew they would be furious. I put it off for as long as I dared, but I finally had to choose a date and go with it. I chose Friday, Jan. 20, 2012. As the date neared, the pressure had risen to an enormous level, and I was dying inside.

My first wife and I had decided to get a divorce right before I left for Afghanistan in late 2010. Since I had returned in late 2011, we had been working through the process of dividing up our lives and trying to agree on the legal documents to make it final.

As anyone who has been through a divorce knows, it is an excruciating, horrible, and emotionally destructive process for both parties. I was in a dark, painful place in those final hours before I had to expose myself. Just before "D-Day," as I called it, when I would first tell a general at the Pentagon what was about to happen, I wrote of my emotional state in my journal:

> *It would be a significant understatement to suggest I am presently bankrupt of emotional energy; I am as one lying in a crumpled heap, naked, on a cold, damp, concrete floor. Alone. I tried to go to sleep last night without assistance and went to bed around 10:30 p.m. But I awoke about two hours later in an unpleasant place: I was saturated with a sense of fear.*
>
> *I don't know for sure what I was afraid of, but as best I can describe the feeling it was something like experiencing the presence of evil in my room—and I was honestly scared. I got up and took some Tylenol PM to help me sleep and thank God the pills did their work not too long after that.*

I was restless that entire Friday. My heart was racing in my chest. I didn't want to eat anything. The hour I had chosen to make the move had finally arrived. I will never forget the exhilarating thrill and sheer terror of the moment as I walked across the Pentagon to drop off the classified report with the inspector general, and then to the office of the Army's vice chief of staff, Gen. Peter Chiarelli.

I had worked for General Chiarelli in the Pentagon when he was assigned there as a two-star general during my 2003-05 tenure working in the Army Operation Center (AOC). He was mere days from retiring and I had set an appointment, ostensibly to wish him well. When I got to his office he greeted me warmly and seemed genuinely happy to see me. I didn't waste much time.

"Sir," I said firmly and clearly, "you may not be so pleased when you hear what I have to tell you." The smile mostly left his face and he asked me to continue. I explained all that had happened during my Afghan deployment and about the classified report I had just submitted to the IG, and finally about the AFJ and The New York Times pieces that would be published on Feb. 5. I also gave him a printed full copy of a detailed 86-page unclassified document I had written so he could read as much as he cared to read (a <u>leaked copy</u> was later published online).

I was deeply relieved at what happened next. Though I had had great respect for General Chiarelli, I knew he could be a tough task-master and I had seen him verbally eviscerate people during his time as director of the AOC. I prepared myself to receive full vent from him. Instead, he was very cordial, seemed somewhat sympathetic to my findings, and in the end, said he wasn't sure what was going to happen next. I thanked him for his time and graciousness and left.

My direct boss at the Rapid Equipping Force was a full colonel and typically soft-spoken, but with a powerful personality. He and I had never been close, and he seemed to generally dislike me. But when I told him, he too, was more restrained than I had anticipated.

Other generals on the Army staff, however, were indeed furious and felt I had been disloyal. I vehemently disagreed, so their feelings didn't do any particular harm to me. Because of the whistleblower protections for government employees—and because members of Congress had expressed support for me—Army leaders in the Pentagon were forbidden from taking any action that might imply retribution for telling the truth. That turned out to be both good and bad.

It was good in that it meant I would not lose my job or be charged with anything frivolous (though, to be clear, I had scrupulously followed every Army rule and regulation to ensure I didn't give anyone a chance to charge me with any wrongdoing). But it was bad in that I had to go to the Pentagon every day and sit at a desk just outside where the generals worked, knowing that some of them hated the sight of me.

As the days passed from my disclosure to the day the two articles would be publicly released, the full eight hours of every workday were hugely stressful: I was persona non grata to virtually all my bosses; even my coworkers were afraid to be seen talking to me. I eventually got out of the Pentagon and arranged another posting elsewhere in Washington.

Finally, the day of publication arrived, and on Sunday morning The New York Times article ran with the headline, "In Afghan War, Officer Becomes a Whistle-blower," and the Armed Forces Journal published my work with the title, "Truth, Lies, and Afghanistan." I wish the Times had chosen a different headline: I didn't consider myself a "whistleblower" but a truth-teller. Still, it was gratifying that the newspaper had considered the report worthy of such prominent display.

In the days that followed, I was interviewed by Barbara Starr on CNN, Margaret Warner on PBS *Newshour*, and others. I gave unofficial briefings on Capitol Hill to members of Congress and their staff, shared my story with other journalists, and in April was honored with the Ridenhour Truth Telling Prize. But when assessing the results of my efforts, probably the most illuminating example was what happened at the Pentagon press briefing three days after my report went public.

As it turned out, the three-star general in charge of U.S. ground troops in Afghanistan, Lt. Gen. Curtis Scaparrotti, was at the Pentagon for some business and had a scheduled press conference for Wednesday, Feb. 8. After his opening statement, Scaparrotti was asked by Bob Burns of the Associated Press whether he had seen my report and what he thought about it. "I read the article," the general answered, and "what I would say is this: It's one person's view."

He went on to say he had spoken to many soldiers and that while my observations may have been real, he suggested that they were limited. Ultimately, Scaparrotti said, "I'm confident that—in my personal view that our outlook is accurate." He also reinforced everything Petraeus and other generals had said—that we were on the right path, that things were improving—and that ultimately our strategy would succeed. And that was it. The press conference continued to other questions and almost no one asked follow-up questions after that day.

Of course, the president didn't listen to me; the Pentagon refuted what I had said; and after a short bump in the media, everyone shrugged their shoulders and moved on. The war continued, also without change, and it was as if I had never said a word.

Scaparrotti was wrong at that February briefing and the war ground on pointlessly on during his assignment. He was rewarded for his "loyalty" in conveying the popular version of events by eventually being promoted to a four-star general and given the prestigious position of <u>Supreme Allied Commander, Europe</u>. Petraeus was wrong with his optimistic assessment made at his March 2011 hearing. He was rewarded for his deception by being selected <u>as director</u> of the Central Intelligence Agency (<u>before resigning</u> in disgrace after <u>sharing classified materials</u> with his mistress).

Hundreds of other Americans, on the other hand, were not rewarded. In the eight years since my report went public, several hundred more troops have been killed. Thousands more have been wounded. The Afghan army remains a minimally capable military force. The Afghan government remains hopelessly divided and corrupt. The Taliban remain ascendant. The Pakistani government continues to support the insurgency.

In short, nothing of the positive outcomes these many leaders predicted came to pass while all the problems I warned them about continue to fester.

How many more Americans must die before our leaders admit the utter failure and painful futility of our war in Afghanistan, recognize it can never be won on a battlefield, and end the war? This conflict

Davis on patrol in Kunar

should have been brought to a close in 2012 when I pointed out the numerous fundamental reasons why it *couldn't* be won militarily. Had it been ended then, we would have saved a terrible fate for thousands of American service members and saved hundreds of billions of taxpayer dollars.

Our country would still be safe from future terror attacks – as we have always been, with or without combat troops on the ground in Afghanistan—and we would long ago have cut loose the anchor of our failure in Afghanistan.

For those who may still believe that to withdraw from Afghanistan would increase the threat of "a new 9/11," I will relieve you of those fears in the next chapter. The short answer: Afghanistan was only marginally associated with the planning of the 2001 attacks, and we have greatly expanded and improved our ability to defend against any future attacks *no matter where on the globe they originate*. This capability is not dependent on having ground troops stationed in Afghanistan—or anywhere abroad.

Chapter 5: *How to Safely End the Forever-war in Afghanistan*

So where do we go from here? I've described in the preceding chapters how during the past two decades even some of America's most senior uniformed and civilian leaders—all the way up to and including generals and presidents—have lied to the American people to protect their cherished plans and wars. These leaders have told the public whatever they felt necessary to prevent the people from demanding an end to failed wars.

Too many powerful men and women at the highest levels of our government remain consumed with portraying the fiction that every action with which they are associated—even those that have been demonstrable failures—as being the right one.

They may be unwilling to make changes or admit a course of action has failed out of a belief they will be personally blamed or fail to get reelected. That fear is not without merit: If a leader fails enough (or fails to a significant enough level), they may well be replaced or defeated in the next election.

But here's the thing: *I don't care*. Leadership isn't supposed to be a plum job that benefits the office-holder, but a position of responsibility and service to the people.

It is appropriate that substandard performers be replaced by others who can get the job done, especially where national security is concerned, and lives are literally on the line. It should be an article of faith that senior government leaders (whether elected or appointed) or serve in the armed forces are first and foremost, *public servants*. These positions are about serving the needs of American citizens, about making the country better, about making everyone safe, secure, and free.

That's what they *should* be about, anyway. What we *have* right now, most regrettably, is a system in which the greatest measure of success is leaders' ability to hold on to their jobs. The most prominent posts are too often awarded to those who look good on TV and have a keen ability to demonize their opponents—actual performance is often relegated to the margins.

As this book has sought to graphically point out, this propensity of our senior leaders towards self-aggrandizement is not victim-free. There is no greater example of how this harms American interests than the war in Afghanistan.

By all rights, leaders with even average skills should have brought that war to a close more than a decade ago (*excellent* leaders would have ended it in the summer of 2002). Instead, leader after leader has willfully maintained the fiction that things were on the right path.

In that decade of deception, thousands of American women and men were killed in Afghanistan, tens of thousands of others wounded, and hundreds of thousands suffered traumatic brain injuries or post-traumatic stress disorder. You read that right: The total of U.S. killed, wounded, and injured in Afghanistan is measured in the *hundreds of thousands*.

One of the primary national security objectives of the next administration—whether Trump or Biden—should be to stop paying exorbitant prices in American blood and treasure to support policies that can only fail. It's absurd what we've been doing for decades: *paying to fail with the bodies of hundreds of thousands of Americans and trillions of taxpayer dollars*.

The most pressing foreign policy imperative facing the incoming administration will be the one in most urgent need of corrective action: ending our many forever-wars, starting with the 19-years-and-counting debacle in Afghanistan.

The White House should take action to end the war and professionally withdraw all our troops, in a reasonable time frame, and in coordination with our allies in Kabul and NATO. On Sept 9, 2020 Trump tweeted, "LET'S BRING THEM HOME!" in response to a segment by Fox News' Tucker Carlson, "Trump Wants Troops Out of the Middle East." As of this writing, unfortunately, Trump's declaration did not mean he planned to end the Afghan war.

In a press conference earlier that same day, Gen. Kenneth F. McKenzie, selected by Trump to head Central Command, told Pentagon reporters that he had been given no withdrawal order. The president ordered McKenzie to reduce the number of troops in Afghanistan, he said, "to 4,500 and I've received no orders to go below that at this time."

Though that number of troops will be the lowest number since December 2001, it is still not a withdrawal and will merely extend the war, albeit at the cost of a lower level of pointless waste. The bigger problem is that by keeping the mission active, it will be easy at any point for Trump or a President Biden to merely order the deployment of more troops. McKenzie laid the foundation for that possibility at the press conference.

The general's continuing mission, he explained, was to make sure "that neither al-Qaida nor ISIS [have] the ability to generate in ungoverned spaces attacks against the homeland of the United States or those of our allies and partners." He claimed he could accomplish that task with 4,500 troops. I served on the ground in Afghanistan at the height of the Obama surge in 2010—when there were 140,000 U.S. and NATO troops deployed—and I can confirm that there were major portions of the country that were beyond the ability of our troops to control.

It should be laughable to suggest that a minuscule force of 4,500 could do so now. The biggest truth to understand, however, is that we don't need to control terrain in Afghanistan to keep the American homeland safe from terror attacks. Suggesting we don't need to physically control territory in Afghanistan to keep us safe flies in the face of conventional wisdom—but conventional wisdom is wrong. Here's why.

As has been the case for decades, some of the most notorious and vocal defenders of the forever war in Afghanistan claim that ending the war there would invite a new 9/11, that a withdrawal would be "indefensible" and would sacrifice all we have built there, that our efforts there are succeeding and we just need to give it more time. Evidence overwhelmingly proves none of these claims are accurate.

The initial strategic objectives President George W. Bush gave the military to accomplish in October 2001 were reasonable, attainable, and limited: Destroy Al-Qaeda's presence in Afghanistan and punish the Taliban for hosting them. By late spring of the following year, the Taliban were driven from power and Al-Qaeda's membership was decimated.

Had Bush been willing to take the win and withdraw the troops, we could have saved our country hundreds of billions of dollars and the lives and limbs of tens of thousands of American troops. Instead, he changed the mission to nation-building—inviting disastrous consequences.

In 2007, Bush unveiled a new strategy in which he said the U.S. would help the Afghan government "establish a stable, moderate, and democratic state that respects the rights of its citizens, governs its territory effectively, and is a reliable ally in this war against extremists and terrorists." That mission was militarily unattainable and locked us into a no-win situation. When he first took office, Obama dug the hole deeper and proved content to passively ride out the status quo until he could pass it off to Trump.

Trump had long lobbied to withdraw from Afghanistan before winning the 2016 election, but the biggest impediment to his making good on that solid instinct has been influential beltway insiders—in Congress, from certain think tanks, and self-proclaimed foreign policy experts in the media—raised in the mold of Cold Warriors, expecting or even inviting perpetual warfare.

One such influencer has been Sen. Lindsey Graham, a Republican from South Carolina, who publicly told Trump that if he withdrew from Afghanistan, "there will be another 9/11." That fear is based on a significant lack of understanding of how the original 9/11 was developed and inadequate knowledge of the powerful global tools at Trump's disposal to keep us safe from *any* new terrorist strike. Once you understand that the country of Afghanistan was only marginally relevant to the September 2001 attacks, it becomes easier to understand why a full withdrawal now will not materially affect our national security.

The "safe haven" myth

Graham is only the most prominent of a long line of influential opinion-makers who have warned that withdrawing U.S. forces from Afghanistan would create a "safe haven" from which terrorists could plan and operate. But Afghanistan is not and never has been unique in its potential to host terrorists. That myth has had a stranglehold on reasonable policy since 2001 and has since helped to sink every attempt at ending the war.

The truth is that the U.S. retains the capability to destroy terrorists globally, including in Afghanistan, without a permanent military ground presence. It is instructive to examine how this myth got started, why it has held for so many years, and how to shut it down so we can start using the military in ways that keep us safe and doesn't dissipate its strength in pointless missions abroad.

Following the 2001 terror attacks, the U.S. rightly sought to dismantle global terrorist organizations and punish those who had protected or tolerated Al-Qaeda. The initial U.S. campaign in Afghanistan did just that, overthrowing the Taliban government and decimating Al-Qaeda.

But U.S. strategists learned the wrong lessons from 9/11, believing that a U.S.-friendly government in Kabul was necessary to prevent future anti-American terrorism originating out of Afghanistan. This led to a 19-years-and-counting nation-building effort that has failed to yield any lasting successes while imposing massive on-going costs to the American people.

The misapprehension that hinders U.S. counterterrorism policy is the idea that hostile states and "failed states"—those in which the government lacks a monopoly on violence within its borders—provide terrorists "safe haven" to attack the U.S. or other Western countries. Supporters of continuing the war in Afghanistan argue that the terrorist attacks of 2001 happened because Afghanistan lacked effective governance, allowing Al-Qaeda to openly plot its evil deed.

Any U.S. withdrawal without a strong pro-American national government in Kabul, many advocates claimed, would presumably allow the Taliban to overthrow the Afghan government and recreate the conditions that spawned the attacks in the first place. Such a reading of the history leading up to the September 2001 attacks is fatally flawed.

Nation-building and counterterrorism are distinct goals, and the failures that made 9/11 possible did not directly stem from political disorder in Afghanistan. Instead, 9/11 occurred because the U.S. underestimated the threat terrorists posed, made half-hearted efforts to disrupt their networks abroad, and failed to implement effective homeland security measures when we had the chance.

Washington had multiple opportunities to eliminate Osama bin Laden before 2001 but declined, believing the risks of a strike outweighed the benefits. And although Afghanistan was serving as a base of operations for Al-Qaeda at the time of the 2001 attacks, the attacks themselves were planned from several countries—with key terrorists planning and preparing openly *within the United States itself.*

The implications of this reality are clear and stark: even if al-Qaeda didn't have a base of operations in Afghanistan, the operational preparations would have been made and the attack conducted regardless.

The U.S. for decades has been capable of locating and killing hostile individuals abroad through aerial surveillance, robust on-the-ground intelligence connections, and global strike technology. This capability, always considerable, has been substantially enhanced since 9/11.

The political will of the U.S. to pursue terrorists and their enablers is also unquestionable; the aggressive and voluminous counterterrorism measures we've conducted in the past two decades have made that clear. But it is past time to reject the false idea, deeply engrained in the U.S.

for years, that if we "abandon" Afghanistan, we'll suffer a new terror attack.

Afghanistan was not necessary to carry out 9/11

In 2009, President Obama ordered the first of what would be two major troop surges that year, arguing that, "[i]f the Afghan government falls to the Taliban—or allows Al-Qaeda to go unchallenged—that country will again be a base for terrorists who want to kill as many of our people as they possibly can."

Nine years later, President Trump's Secretary of Defense James Mattis would offer a similar argument: that the U.S. was in Afghanistan to prevent it from being a launching pad for transnational terrorism, that we could not leave until the Afghan military was self-sufficient, and that such an exit was possible only after the Afghan government and Taliban had concluded a peace agreement.

But much of the groundwork for the original 9/11 attacks was laid outside Afghanistan. The most definitive account of how the initial 9/11 plot was conceived, planned, and prepared comes from the 9/11 Commission Report ("the Report") published in 2004.

As the 9/11 Commission lays out in painstaking detail, Afghanistan was incidental to the attack's planning. Khalid Shaik Muhammed (KSM) began conceiving the attack as far back as 1993 while living in Qatar. A key collaborator with whom KSM worked, Ramzi Yousef, was based in the Philippines.

Al-Qaeda was still a fledgling, not-ready-for-prime-time organization in the early 1990s, and according to the report, the early planning for what would later be the 9/11 attack was not even an Al-Qaeda operation. Rather, it was something KSM was hoping Bin Laden would approve and turn into an Al-Qaeda mission.

After initially fighting against the Soviets in Afghanistan and being marginally allied with the U.S., bin Laden turned increasingly hostile toward the West after the war's end. By 1994, Saudi Arabia stripped him of his citizenship, and bin Laden went to Sudan in exile. In mid-1996, bin Laden moved his operations from Sudan to Afghanistan, later followed by KSM, and in "late 1998 to early 1999, planning for the 9/11 operation began in earnest," the report said.

While Afghanistan is associated with 9/11 because it served as bin Laden's residence, the attack was conceived, planned, and executed by Al-Qaeda members operating out of *numerous* countries. KSM, the mastermind of the plot, formed his initial concept between 1993 and 1996 while living and traveling in Sudan, Yemen, Malaysia, and Brazil. After the single meeting with bin Laden in Tora Bora in 1996, he refined his plan in India, Indonesia, Malaysia, and Pakistan.

Afghanistan is by no means unique in its ability to host terrorists. Had bin Laden continued living in Sudan, his planning could have happened there — or just as easily taken place in Pakistan, Malaysia, Chechnya, the Philippines, or other nations that had active Al-Qaeda cells. In fact, a majority of the key operational planning and rehearsing was not conducted in Afghanistan at all, but in Germany; the most important training took place in the U.S. itself.

The 9/11 plot was conceived by a group of internationally mobile terrorists with access to hideouts in several countries, and its operation grew out of a permissive security environment for terrorism worldwide. There was nothing special about Afghanistan. Global vigilance against terrorism is appropriate regardless of the country in which our enemies reside, Afghanistan included. We must recognize, however, that occupying tiny portions of individual countries does *nothing* to prevent terror attacks here.

Even under Taliban control, Afghanistan-based terrorists were never outside our reach

Even before 9/11, the U.S. possessed the intelligence-gathering and targeting capability to locate and kill key terrorists (including bin Laden) anywhere in the world. It's worth noting, however, that while a figure like bin Laden is uniquely dangerous and his death would have been a blow to Al-Qaeda, there is no guarantee it would have stopped the 9/11 attacks.

On Aug. 7, 1998, U.S. embassies in Tanzania and Kenya were bombed, killing 224 people and wounding more than 5,000. Less than two weeks later, President Bill Clinton ordered a retaliatory strike against suspected terrorist bases in Afghanistan and Sudan, hoping to kill bin Laden, the bombing's mastermind. When it became clear bin Laden survived, the U.S. on Nov. 4, 1998, charged him with 224 counts of murder, and the CIA began aggressively seeking opportunities to kill or capture him.

In February 1999, the CIA had detailed intelligence that pinpointed the location of bin Laden at an isolated hunting camp in the desert near Kandahar. The trigger was never pulled because of political concerns in the White House. At the time, the administration believed the risks of a successful strike outweighed the benefits.

In May 1999, the U.S. got its at least third—and last—chance to eliminate bin Laden before 9/11. "CIA assets in Afghanistan reported on bin Laden's location in and around Kandahar," the 9/11 report stated. Yet again senior officials in the CIA and Pentagon were reluctant to authorize the strike—and the chance to kill bin Laden was lost for the last time. A CIA official directly involved in the operations expressed anger at "having a chance to get [bin Laden] three times in 36 hours and foregoing the chance each time."

The report notes nine separate decision points between 1998 and 2000 where a different approach might have allowed U.S. or U.S.-backed forces to kill bin Laden. The problem was not a lack of capability, but the fact that policymakers chose not to proceed. Today, the U.S. possesses substantial motivation and capability to hunt terrorists wherever they take refuge, and technological progress (like the development of drone platforms) makes it more feasible than ever.

These episodes demonstrate that there is no basis to claims made by officials from multiple administrations that troops on the ground in Afghanistan are necessary to keep us safe at home. Despite having no forces in Afghanistan before 2001, we cultivated the intelligence necessary to locate the leader behind the 9/11 plot and created nine opportunities to kill him before the homeland was attacked. Our ability to identify and take out direct threats to our country—no matter where in the world they may originate—has only increased in the two decades since 9/11.

Counterinsurgency Operations to Defend Kabul not Counterterror Campaigns to Protect America

Despite claims to the contrary, the overriding mission of the U.S. military in Afghanistan since 2002 has not been counterterror operations designed to keep America safe. Rather, it has been counterinsurgency designed to keep the government in Kabul safe. But the U.S. armed forces do not exist to keep foreign governments permanently in power. They exist to keep the citizens of *our* country safe. The fact that American men and women who faithfully serve our country in uniform have been required for so many years to sacrifice their lives for another government should upset every American.

Policymakers in the past three administrations assumed states with hostile, weak, or no governments are breeding grounds for terrorism, and that the only way to prevent terrorists from operating freely would be to create a friendly, effective government from scratch. To that end, the U.S. sought to prop up Kabul at all costs. Unlike President Bush's original set of objectives, however, this mission is not only unnecessary but also virtually impossible to accomplish, requiring the military to build a unified, well-ordered society where none had previously existed. Nearly 18 years after we started fighting in Afghanistan, the Taliban hold more territory than at any point since 2001, and the Afghan government remains unpopular, corrupt, and dependent on foreign aid. Our military is simply not suited for the nation-building task at hand.

Taliban recruitment is largely driven by disaffected Pashtuns angry at Kabul's corruption and incompetence and at what they see as a U.S. occupation of their homeland. Fortunately, the Taliban have shown no appetite for engaging in anti-American terrorism outside of Afghanistan and are hostile to more radical groups, such as ISIS.

Even at the peak of the U.S. presence in Afghanistan, there were substantial parts of the country that the U.S. did not patrol, let alone control. During the 2010–2014 Afghan surge, there were as many as

140,000 U.S. and NATO troops in-country, yet they could not achieve a lasting victory. That is no surprise considering how much nation-building demands of the military. No amount of acceptable force, short of widespread, brutal repression, is sufficient for remaking a nation hobbled by poverty, corruption, and infighting into a modern, well-run state.

While U.S. troops can prevent Kabul from falling as long as they remain, they cannot make Afghan politicians govern effectively, force the Afghan army and police units to protect their people without preying on them, compel the various tribes and warlords to work together or eradicate the opium trade. Nation-building has been an unequivocal failure, and all evidence indicates a continued U.S. presence—no matter how large or permanent—would yield no better outcomes than what we have already achieved. If anything, extending our presence could lead to exiting under even worse conditions than today. Applying an external military solution to internal political, cultural, and religious problems will never succeed. Fortunately, U.S. security isn't contingent on succeeding at this venture.

The U.S. doesn't need to occupy foreign nations to fight terrorism

The U.S. can project power globally via aircraft carriers, strategic lift from the Air Force and Navy, and the Army's ability to launch operations from those platforms. The U.S. military's ISR-Strike system, merging robust global intelligence operations, high-tech surveillance, and strike capabilities, along with skilled field operatives and local assets on the ground, have protected the U.S. homeland. Our ability to locate terrorists hiding in remote locations and conduct strikes to eliminate them has only improved since 9/11, as graphically demonstrated in the 2011 operation that killed Osama bin Laden in Pakistan, the 2018 strike on ISIS leader Abu Bakr al-Baghdadi in Syria, and the 2020 raid to kill the leader of Al-Qaeda in the Arabian Peninsula in Yemen. No place on Earth is beyond our reach.

The U.S. ISR-Strike is composed of systems that integrate and process information from a wide variety of sources, satellites, and other tools to monitor potential threats in real time and weapons systems that can be deployed <u>to strike targets</u> once a decision has been made. A major portion of the <u>$60-70 billion</u> spent annually on intelligence in the U.S. is invested in this capability. In addition to the intelligence community, the military has also developed its own ISR-Strike tools, with the Air Force alone operating 425 manned and unmanned aircraft of <u>14 different types</u> dedicated to that purpose.

Once intelligence identifies a threat, if no other method exists to eliminate or disrupt it, unmanned aerial vehicles can track its location and launch strikes without putting American lives at risk. Advances in drone technology, including better imaging and the ability to linger over an area longer, have made drones a potent counterterrorism tool. Abu Musab al-Zarqawi, a leading terrorist in Iraq in 2005, was located after the U.S. deployed <u>dozens of drones</u> to aerially scout the streets of Fallujah.

The ability to launch strikes from a variety of platforms and long-range bombers enables the U.S. to eliminate targets far from where it maintains a military presence. A successful bombing raid on 90 ISIS fighters in the Libyan desert in 2012, carried out by aircraft launched from Missouri, is one of <u>many examples</u>.

Even the 2019 mission to kill al-Baghdadi featured a strike force that <u>originated well outside</u> the country. Following al-Baghdadi's death, Marine Gen. Kenneth F. McKenzie <u>briefed reporters</u> that the mission was neither contingent nor dependent on having troops in Syria: "The United States military has the capability to go almost anywhere and support ourselves, even at great distances, so that was not a limiting factor."

Neither will it be a limiting factor for any future direct threat to our security—irrespective of whether we have troops on the ground.

What We Should Do Now

The two decades we have been at war in Afghanistan have proven futile. The war will never be "won" with military means because the problems plaguing Afghanistan are political and ethnic, not military.

Attempting to remake Afghanistan—or any foreign state—in our image does not mitigate the threat of terrorism. If anything, trying to compel adherence to our preferred political system exacerbates the problem and unwittingly adds fuel to the fire of radicals.

American security is best served by ending our existing open-ended military commitments, withdrawing our troops from ongoing counterinsurgency and nation-building conflicts in Afghanistan, and relying on our remarkable ability to project power anywhere on the globe to keep us safe. It's time to dispel with the "safe haven" myth, end the war in Afghanistan, and secure America by pursuing an effective counterterrorism policy.

The best thing our government can do to preserve national security and financial prosperity is to end the war and conduct a quick, professional withdrawal, closely coordinated with our allies. Leaving may indeed cause a spike in violence in Afghanistan—but staying will perversely maintain the violence while perpetually draining America of blood and treasure. It's time to recognize reality and end the war.

Chapter 6: *A Foreign Policy that Makes Sense – and Profit*

After the United States defeated Saddam Hussein's forces in 1991 and emerged the victor in the Cold War less than two years later, our safety as a nation was as secure as any has ever been throughout world history. Our forces were strong, our economy powerful, and (excluding nuclear weapons) our potential adversaries benign. Sept. 11 wrecked that dynamic.

Though not for all the reasons you might expect.

After our initial response to the 2001 terror attacks, we had the opportunity to maintain global military supremacy and expand our economic and security well-being. Instead, our leaders squandered that opportunity— equally during Republican and Democratic Administrations.

Rather than responding in prudent, measured, and responsible ways to the actual threats, we imagined enemies in every corner of the globe, embarking on what remains to this day a self-destructive, global forever-war. Far from making us more secure, these many pointless and perpetual conflicts have drained our economy of trillions of dollars, resulting in the shameful sacrifice of the lives, health, and well-being of *hundreds of thousands* of our servicemen and women.

More troubling for the long haul, forever-wars have produced the twin maladies of increasing anger and hatred toward our country among potential enemies, and doubt and resentment among our closest allies. Regardless of whether Donald Trump wins a second term or Joe Biden comes out on top this November, America needs to dramatically reorient its foreign policy in a way that increases our national security and optimizes our ability to prosper economically.

That reorientation is desperately needed because since 9/11, both Republican and Democratic administrations and Congresses have routinely based their foreign policies, not on rational, logical, and sober analysis of the world as it is, but on fanning often-irrational (and emotionally sensitive) fear.

From the end of World War II through the conclusion of the Cold War, America's guiding foreign policy philosophy had been realism. After the trauma of 9/11, we abandoned that concept and replaced it with one predicated on seemingly contradictory factors: fear and conceit.

In the arrogant belief that we were bullet-proof internationally, we abandoned almost all restraint and took action everywhere our desires led, failing to consider the ramifications of our actions, believing such actions to be unnecessary.

We didn't need to, many seemed to believe, because we had unrivaled military and economic strength. But our leaders couldn't openly expand into wars and routinely threaten the use of military action to achieve their preferred policy goals—they needed to keep the support of the population by keeping them in a steady-state of fear.

Today's foreign policy establishment tells us to fear a constantly expanding (and often rotating) raft of fears. We are told we must perpetually fear terrorism, must fear the Russians could attack at any moment; must fear that China is seeking global domination at our expense; we are told we have to be afraid of Iran, North Korea, Cuba, Venezuela. But are those fears valid?

If a sober and comprehensive analysis were to reveal a given country or group had both the capacity and intent to attack the United States or our vital national interests, then we should by all means strongly deter that opponent—and if enemy actions forced war on us, to decisively crush that threat.

If, on the other hand, that same detailed analysis revealed that any given potential adversary doesn't have both the capacity *and* the will to attack us (both are necessary to represent a substantial threat), then a different level of deterrence would be appropriate. Three cases can illustrate.

Scenario one: let's say Country A is an unfriendly competitor of the U.S. and has the military capacity to launch a successful air, land, and sea attack on our country or military stationed abroad. While Country A dislikes the U.S., they have nevertheless made no threats against us, and beyond fielding a deterrent force, have taken no actions against our troops, homeland, or global interests.

In such a case, our government would be obligated to ensure our sea and air fleets are on constant vigil, that our land forces are well-equipped and ready, and that we maintain a high level of combat readiness throughout the armed forces to meet any future attack.

Scenario two: Country B dislikes the U.S., has a regionally robust military, and has threatened to attack our country or treaty partners. Neither America nor our allies have taken any action against Country B, and if it made good on its threat, the attack against us would be unprovoked and unwarranted.

In this scenario, it makes sense to field a strong, well-equipped, and trained U.S. military, and depending on the conditions, might also warrant the deployment of strong demonstration forces in the region near the would-be opponent; exhibiting powerful resolve is a cost-effective way to deter an aggressive enemy short of war by making the aggressors realize they would pay an excessive price and lose in a fight against us.

Scenario three: Country C hates us but cannot make good on its threat against our globally deployed armed forces or the U.S. homeland. We should still pay close attention to them, constantly monitor them through our global intelligence, surveillance, and reconnaissance networks, but otherwise not divert any combat power to perpetual deployment.

We would continue to maintain the same robust air, land, and sea forces to defend our homeland, make good on our treaty obligations, and ensure our troops maintain an adequately high level of combat readiness.

Our existing military, along with our unmatched ability to project power around the globe, is sufficient to deter weaker aggressors from taking rash actions. If they did try, we have sufficient power to crush them quickly.

These three scenarios could apply to virtually any country in the world today. It is key to note that the common denominator is the requirement for the U.S. to always maintain a strong, properly-funded, and well-trained military. There is utility, however, in examining how the dynamics portrayed in the three scenarios have played out in history.

In the leadup to World War II, there was much physical evidence that Hitler had powerful territorial ambitions in Europe. As early as the mid-1930s, he began a major buildup of armored land forces and modern air forces necessary to invade other countries. Hitler wrote as early as 1924 that he considered other races inferior and that Germany needed "living space" for its people.

Then in 1936 he remilitarized the Rhineland adjacent to France in violation of Treaty of Versailles, absorbed Austria in 1938, occupied Czechoslovakia in Spring 1939, invaded Poland in September 1939, and finally even conquered France in 1940. History has not been kind to British Prime Minister Neville Chamberlain whose appeasement at Munich in 1938 removed the final barrier to Hitler's long road to aggression. That entire dynamic is instructive to our foreign policy today.

If any nation in today's world began a buildup of forces and communicated, directly or indirectly, a desire to conquer the territory of America or our allies—much like Hitler had done by the mid-1930s—we would be within our rights to increase our physical deterrence against such a foe and make certain they realized we were ready, willing, and able to fight them should they foolishly attack us.

The overriding preference is to avoid war, however, by showing tough opponents we mean business and demonstrate both the capacity and resolve to decisively act should any opponent launch an unprovoked attack, say, along the lines of Pearl Harbor. Deterrence and diplomacy are the keys to keeping our country safe.

Based on observed behavior, today's foreign policy practitioners seem to believe the best way to keep us safe is by routinely threatening — and not infrequently using — lethal military power. The results of this mentality should be coming more and more clear to the American public: "Shoot first, talk later" has *increased* the threats our country faces, expended astronomical numbers of dollars to fund it, and provided a poor deterrent.

In cases where we have to deter opponents who possess both the intent and capacity to attack us can be very costly, but under threatening circumstances, it is vital to ensure our country is never left unnecessarily vulnerable. That kind of readiness makes sense.

What *doesn't* make sense, however, is applying that same high level of spending and forward-demonstration of forces to defend against attacks from potential adversaries who don't have the intent or the ability to attack us.

For example, our NATO ally Turkey — which has become increasingly hostile to America in the past half-decade — has a modern military capable of harming American interests in the Middle East. But aside from displeasure at our actions relative to their preferences in Syria, they have demonstrated no *intent* to use that military against us.

It would be an absurd waste of time and treasure to spend tens of billions annually defending against Turkey just because they *may* someday change their minds and turn against us (if that did happen, then a change of policy would be required).

The more pertinent question: what if the country under consideration was a non-friendly nation such as China? If they had a military capable of inflicting great harm to U.S. forces but did not communicate an intent to attack us, would it be wise to spend large amounts of money as though they did represent a late-1930s Nazi-like threat?

The question is complex and of paramount importance to address, but the answer is found in an examination of the overall foreign policy and national security objectives we establish. With the right policies, we need not spend excessive amounts against every hypothetical threat yet can still absolutely assure our security.

Constructive Realism

A careful, comprehensive, and unemotional analysis of the full range of America's soft and hard power, combined with an equally accurate assessment of any given opponent, persuasively argues that there are vastly superior and cost-effective ways to manage the current foreign policy methods that will keep our country safe and prosperous. The best remedy to the bankrupt concept of fear-based policies is the elevation of a new approach, which I call *constructive realism*.

In its most basic form, constructive realism sees the world as it is and creates policies designed to maximize our government's ability to keep American citizens safe while simultaneously building the best relations possible with the range of states and groups around the world. It does not view the world in simple black-and-white, good-and-evil terms—which don't exist outside of movie scripts in any case—but bases its policies on an unemotional assessment of how we may best safeguard our interests.

Constructive realism seeks to affirm and build on any good elements a given country may have while encouraging them to modify behavior that is wrong or counterproductive to our interests and values. It will first seek the good of our country and treaty partners by elevating the role of diplomacy in solving problems. Yet it also recognizes there are Hitler-like types in the world that at some point may not respond to reasonable diplomatic overtures and force will have to be used.

That is why the best deterrence our country can have is to have armed forces capable of invincible national defense, able to repulse any attack and exact such a terrible price on any foe who dares attack us that none will likely ever try. In the unexpected case some do try, we will crush them and win.

Building such an invincible force, however, does not require fielding the ability to launch offensive operations almost simultaneously against every conceivable foe or perpetually engaging in combat operations against every potential terror threat. That's what we've been trying to do—and annually failing in the attempt—for years now.

The current U.S. policy is to aggressively seek to suppress Russia and China by permanently deploying <u>hundreds of thousands</u> of troops—along with hundreds of aircraft and ships—in Europe and Asia. We fight a host of forever-wars that can never be won in such places as Syria, Iraq, Afghanistan, Yemen, and dozens of locations throughout Africa. We employ coercive diplomacy and threaten to use "any means necessary" against North Korea and Iran. Of late we also, out of irrational fear, threaten poor and destitute Venezuela and Cuba.

Not one of these actions serves American interests.

All of them expend enormous amounts of money, cost the lives of countless U.S. servicewomen and men, and keep the risk of stumbling into unnecessary wars pointlessly high. It weakens our ability to fight wars that may someday be forced on us by peer or near-peer adversaries by dissipating our strength all over the globe in a needlessly broad range of missions. And it diverts hundreds of billions of dollars annually that could better be utilized at home—or simply not spent, limiting the weight on our <u>already-huge</u> national debt.

To be effective in the typically chaotic and complex world, constructive realism must have a set of core values and beliefs that are used to guide the establishment of a set of strategic objectives. America's core values should be those necessary for the government to fulfill its most sacred duties: defend its citizens, secure the rights and liberties of individual citizens, and foster economic conditions that maximize our ability to prosper as a nation.

To support these core values, at a minimum we should establish and maintain the following strategic objectives:

1) provide for the common defense by maintaining a powerful, modern, and properly funded armed forces that can protect against attack from any opponent;

2) prioritize diplomacy in our relations with other global players, seeking win-win outcomes wherever possible;

3) seek peace and stability to the maximum extent possible to support conditions facilitating perpetual economic prosperity.

To accomplish these objectives, senior leaders must conduct an unemotional assessment of the strengths and weaknesses of various foreign entities, ascertain whether they intend to be cooperative, antagonistic, or neutral towards the U.S., and compare that with America's military, diplomatic, and economic capabilities. Our leaders will then be able to select appropriate policies for individual actors to best accomplish each of our objectives. Here's what that could look like in the real world.

Conventional, establishment Washington thinking holds that the greatest threats to U.S. national security today are Iran, North Korea, Russia, and China. The prevailing theory is that the only language these countries understand is brute force, and thus we routinely communicate our willingness to use force against any adversary to compel compliance with our policy preferences. While that sounds tough to many, it has utterly failed to improve either our security or economic well-being. It doesn't take much examination to understand why.

What should be obvious is that neither individuals nor governments react positively to constant threats. If we incessantly demonstrate our willingness to use force to get our way, the result too often is to *harden* an adversary's resolve, not convert or compel them to our way of thinking. No one in the world doubts our ability and willingness to use lethal military force—the large number of our current and perpetual wars confirm this.

Perversely, not only does this overreliance on the military fail to bend opponents to our will, it weakens our deterrent capacity as we become overextended around the world. In short, our current foreign policy based on fear continues to harm our national security and blunts our ability to prosper. There is, however, a superior alternative.

This new strategy takes the world as it is—the messy, the good, the bad, and the "it's complicated"—and provides genuine global leadership that will dramatically reduce the number of wars we fight, reduce the chances we'll get into new ones, and substantially increase the opportunities for prosperity.

Freed from the burdens of constantly fighting and threatening wars, our military will be able to enact badly needed reform and reorganization, resulting in a force that is more capable of defending our country than any since 1991's Desert Storm. We will then be able to focus more energy and activity on expanding and deepening economic development.

Central to forming a sound foreign policy is the recognition that today's global environment is no longer like the one that existed during the Cold War when most of our current security relationships were formed.

For example, NATO was <u>created in 1949</u> under the still-smoldering wreckage of World War II and as the massive Soviet menace was just beginning to rise. Our military presence in <u>South Korea and Japan</u> was solidified in the 1953 aftermath of the Korean War.

The juggernaut that was the USSR, however, no longer exists and the dynamics in the Asia-Pacific have shifted dramatically in the past two decades. While the world has dramatically changed, our security relationships have ossified into an inflexible, static attempt to hold on to the past. It's the equivalent of IBM still trying to market mainframe computers to a smart-phone world; Kodak centering its business on selling black-and-white film; Chevrolet bullheadedly making the same cars it did in 1955.

Every one of those companies would have gone out of business decades ago if they hadn't changed with the times. The same is true of foreign policy: if we don't adapt to new and emerging realities, we will one day find ourselves at an unnecessary — and potentially costly — disadvantage.

Through at least the 1980s, America did exactly what was necessary to stay ahead of the changing curves, adjusting to evolving circumstances and technological development. That realistic focus led our government to make some good decisions that kept the peace for decades and facilitated continued economic development. Yet when the world began to radically change 30 years ago, our leaders failed to change with it and have instead clung to the fiction that the same needs and threats exist today as was the case at the end of the Cold War.

The world that was; the one that is now

In the 1950s, our main security concerns were in Europe with the USSR and in the Asia Pacific with China and North Korea. The Soviet Union and Warsaw Pact alliance would eventually boast 50,000 tanks, thousands of warplanes, and thousands of tactical and strategic nuclear weapons.

In 1950, China was a backward nation, a massive peasantry, and had a large but technologically inferior military; its economy was agrarian-based <u>and tiny</u>. They could <u>swarm 300,000 troops</u> into North Korea to stave off defeat for Pyongyang, but they posed little threat to anyone beyond their borders.

North Korea was likewise very poor, dependent on the USSR and China for economic and military support, and aside from a large infantry force and an arsenal of chemical weapons, did not pose a threat of military attack to anyone besides their southern neighbors on the peninsula. These global dynamics have changed dramatically since the Cold War.

The Soviet Union and its massive Red Army no longer exist, replaced by a considerably smaller and less capable Russia. China, no longer with an antiquated military and backward economy, now has a potent regional military with nuclear weapons and an economy that will soon be the largest in the world. North Korea still has an anemic economy but may now have up to 60 nuclear weapons, a few of which may be able to hit targets in the U.S.

To update our foreign policy so it can most effectively create the conditions necessary for America to remain secure, prosperous, and free, we must have an unemotional and balanced understanding of the world as it is today. Step one is to conduct a fact-based assessment of the world's key regions. That means understanding variations of culture, assessing states' behaviors in recent decades, and analyzing the military capabilities of select nations to assess the level of threat they could potentially pose to our economy.

We have to be careful not to engage in *threat-inflation* (believing a given foe is much stronger and capable than they are) or *threat-deflation* (minimizing or ignoring genuine threats). If today's adversaries possess the ability to do us serious harm, we should build a military capable of deterring them from using their power against us and to be able to defeat them if they try.

We should also adopt an updated version of Sun Tzu's <u>famous dictum</u> that "the supreme art of war is to subdue the enemy without fighting," and restore diplomacy to its rightful place as the tool of first choice for dealing with the world.

Toward that end, we should reform the State Department, invest heavily in recruiting, educating, and retaining top diplomatic talent, and place a much higher value on attaining our international objectives through non-military means. A skilled diplomatic corps, backed by a robust military, can markedly improve our security and expand our economic opportunities abroad.

In addition to generally reforming the State Department, there are two specific categories of foreign policy that need to change for America to remain a dominant economic and military power: end the pointless forever-wars and bring our relations and engagement with other powers into line with on-the-ground realities.

Stop the bleeding today by ending Forever-wars

First and foremost, the forever-wars must end. All of them. The world is no longer like the one following the horrific events of September 2001. In the early days following the attacks, Americans were scared another terrorist attack was just over the horizon, and Americans overwhelmingly supported going to war in Afghanistan. They gave only tepid resistance even to losing some of our civil liberties in the provisions that were passed by Congress.

One year later when Bush Administration officials said Saddam was in league with bin Laden and posed a weapons of mass destruction threat to our country, frightened Americans again did not push back, which ultimately led to the disastrous 2003 war in Iraq. We've been paying for the wars that resulted from that passive environment ever since.

The war in Afghanistan never ended and is now on perpetual autopilot, 19 years old and counting. The Iraq war went on for eight inconclusive years before Obama withdrew the troops—and then returned them three years later to prop up the government in Baghdad. As of this writing (September 2020), about 5,000 troops remain fighting a battle in Iraq that isn't ours, and, in any case, can never be won.

Conflicts in Syria, Niger, Libya, Somalia, Yemen, Pakistan, and elsewhere in Africa are virtually all local fights that have only the thinnest of associations with international terror groups—most of which don't pose a direct threat to America. It is sobering to realize that virtually every conflict initiated by Presidents Bush and Obama have continued under Trump.

Despite what many forever-war supporters claim, American security has *never* been improved by fighting these so-called counter-terror operations "over there" so we don't have to "fight them over here." The truth is, only the tiniest sliver of terror groups have the intent, resources, or *ability* to plan and launch terror attacks against the U.S. from their lairs in Iraq, Afghanistan, Syria, Yemen, or the various conflicts in Africa.

However heinous and barbaric ISIS fighters are—and they are despicable—as a group, they cannot plan and execute attacks against America from bases in Syria that our global capacity to launch ISR-Strike operations can't handle.

Virtually every legitimate terror plot that has been thwarted in the past 18 years—regardless of where it has originated—has been interdicted as a result of excellent work among federal, state, and local law enforcement. As was demonstrated in the operation to take out ISIS leader Abu Bakr Al-Baghdadi in 2019, we don't need troops on the ground in any given location to eliminate a direct threat to America.

As discussed in Chapter 6, our security from terror attacks will continue to be preserved by a combination of U.S. law enforcement, robust cooperation between U.S. and allied intelligence services, and a strong intelligence, surveillance, and reconnaissance ability. Together, these assets and capabilities provide a powerful counterterror capacity that allows us to carry out kinetic strikes anywhere in the world direct threats to America are identified—all without having to permanently maintain combat operations on the ground.

Bringing our engagement with competitors and adversaries into line with reality

Our current foreign policy strategy—to the extent there is a coherent policy—is most accurately defined as one that seeks to find and maintain enemies against which we perpetually fight. There appears to be neither a desire nor an attempt to foster a peaceful and prosperous world without war.

It is always easier and requires less thinking and effort to see enemies all over the world, refuse to engage with them, and regularly present them as evil and in need of opposing. Leading with a powerful and menacing military doesn't require our leaders to study other cultures or seek to understand them. That way of thinking considers it a waste of time to contemplate how best to achieve win-win diplomatic outcomes.

Such a mindset is foolish, shortsighted, and deprives our country of the security it deserves and the prosperity it could otherwise achieve.

Committing to doing the hard work of diplomacy and embracing a mindset that seeks the maximum possible good for our country—a core intent of constructive realism—is the best path to maximum security for America.

The status quo reigning in Washington today considers it anathema to even contemplate an outcome that, in any way, results in something positive for China, Russia, North Korea, or Iran. They desire a zero-sum game in which we always benefit in any interaction and the other side always loses.

That is the surest way to ensure we remain in constant friction and dramatically lowers the possibility of ever living in peace. If a competitor knows it has nothing to gain by entering into negotiations with us, it will severely limit their willingness to work constructively with us on a wide range of subjects. We therefore deny ourselves enormous potential to lower tensions with these powers – and lose out on business opportunities for our citizens.

Constructive realism offers a better path forward.

The upcoming sections examine the world as it actually exists in countries or regions of greatest importance to America and offers a better, realistic path to improved relations with each. Heading into this section, however, something bears repeating: a non-negotiable foundational aspect of constructive realism is that we have a well-trained and well-funded military that can provide an invincible national defense.

We will *never* predicate our security on the hopes that some other country is benign, and that no foe will ever surprise us with an unexpected attack. We'll prepare for them to be bad—but give them every opportunity to demonstrate goodwill.

Here, then, is a brief examination of the conditions that underly our relations with four nations that could pose the greatest threat to our security:

Russia:

Without a doubt, Russia has shown a willingness in the past 15 years to use force against neighbors: Georgia in 2008, Crimea in 2014, and Ukraine since 2014. The question for the U.S., however, is to ascertain why Moscow has been belligerent and what implications that has for American security. The easy path is to blindly assume the Kremlin is a power-hungry force anxiously awaiting the first opportunity to attack Western Europe in a Hitler-style land grab. Such thinking locks us into a permanently adversarial relationship with Russia.

If a careful examination revealed a different intent or that Putin's armed forces are not capable of taking such Nazi-esque actions, however, it would require a different response. While evidence does exist that Putin would love to see a revival of the Soviet Empire, there is little to suggest he would seek to obtain it by military conquest—and *much* evidence to conclude he doesn't have the military capacity to do so.

Many point to Russia's war with Georgia in 2008 and military meddling inside Ukraine in 2014 as evidence of their territorial ambitions. But a closer look reveals that Russian actions did not occur in a void and were based largely on fear the West might one day attack Russian territory.

In its April 2008 Summit, NATO declared that the Western alliance "welcomes Ukraine's and Georgia's Euro-Atlantic aspirations for membership in NATO. We agreed today that these countries will become members of NATO." A cursory check of the map shows that Ukraine and Georgia share approximately 1,500 miles of Russia's southwest border. Only four years earlier, the former Warsaw Pact nations of Latvia, Estonia, and Lithuania—two of which also share a border with Russia—were admitted into NATO.

The Russian parliament condemned the 2004 expansion of the military alliance to its border, saying that it would cause Russia to "reconsider its defense strategy" vis-à-vis the West. Four months after NATO's 2008 declaration to expand to Russia's border, Moscow ordered the attack on Georgia, and in 2014 Moscow took advantage of political instability in Ukraine to annex the Crimea and later covertly sent troops into eastern Ukraine to support separatists.

Moscow regards the expansion of NATO to its borders as an existential threat. NATO and Western nations have long claimed NATO membership posed no threat to Russia. We would love for them to believe our assurances and remain passive to the encroachment—but that was always an unrealistic and naïve hope.

I assure you, no American would ever consider it a benign move if Russia made a military alliance with a country on our border; we even react with significant alarm if either Russia or China has any engagement in our *hemisphere*. Yet we press forward with a continual effort to expand NATO and then express shock when Russia takes actions antithetical to our preferences.

It was clearly and unequivocally a violation of international law that Russia attacked Georgia and took military action in Ukraine. The bigger question we must ask, however, is this: was American security enhanced by pressing the NATO alliance directly to the borders of Russia? If we're answering honestly, the unambiguous answer is no. In truth, our security was harmed, and it unnecessarily raised tensions with Moscow. It's not hard to see why Russia would react aggressively to our eastward expansion.

The NATO alliance and America's forward-deployed military maintained the peace in Europe for four full decades during the Cold War. The boundary between the East and the West was split down the middle of Germany, almost 3,500 miles from the Russian border. We faced the Warsaw Pact, which included the Soviet Union and seven nations of Central and Eastern Europe, and boasted more than 50,000 main battle tanks. That threat no longer exists.

In fact, today all seven of the non-USSR members of the Warsaw Pact that used to be allied against the West are now members of NATO, effectively allied against Moscow. Russia itself has only a few thousand tanks — and these are inferior to virtually all the modern tanks of NATO with the notable exception of limited numbers of the Armata tank. In any case, Russia lacks the military infrastructure to support *any* land invasion beyond its borders and into Europe.

Russian military forces are already heavily taxed in maintaining their postures in eastern Ukraine, Crimea, and the two provinces of Georgia. Russia never expanded its territorial grabs beyond the disputed provinces of Georgia and thus far have never moved beyond the fig-leaf claim they aren't officially in eastern Ukraine.

In short, Putin is close to maxed out in maintaining his current level of deployment and however much he may wish to do so, is incapable of successfully conquering European lands. That is not to say Russia isn't capable of putting up a fierce defense of its homeland, however.

There is no necessity to press our military alliance closer and closer to the Russian border when they don't have the physical ability to threaten an invasion of Western territory. Meanwhile, European members of NATO already have a vast superiority over Russia both numerically and in technological superiority.

If we press too hard, however, and insist on advancing closer to the Russian border, we can count on an increasingly belligerent Kremlin and will keep an unnecessarily high level of tensions between our countries—and the risk of accidental war or miscalculation will remain pointlessly high.

Taking the emotions and historical baggage out of the equation, constructive realism's cold and accurate analysis of the security situation between the U.S. and Russia reveals that we can maintain our security with our standard military posture and do not need to press a military alliance to the borders of a comparatively weak Russia.

China:

It is important to understand right up front that China is paranoid of the West, as they have been invaded or exploited by foreigners since at least the start of the Opium Wars of the mid-1800s. In most cases, China was too weak to defend against Western exploitation and suffered as a result. Current Chinese leaders don't intend to be humiliated like that again and remain on a decades-long effort to build a strong national defense.

Beijing has indeed shown a willingness to use force when it feels its interests or survival is threatened. After winning a civil war in 1949, its Communist leaders have vowed to "reunite" Taiwan to the mainland and freely promise to use force if Taiwan declares independence.

Chinese leaders sent 300,000 troops into North Korea to fight the U.S. in 1950, and since then has fought border skirmishes against its neighbors in India (1962), the Soviet Union (1969), Vietnam (1979), and another brief clash against Indian border troops this year. What they have never done, however, is gone abroad to fight another country.

Those facts are key for U.S. policymakers and citizens to understand when forming China policies. If they feel threatened, Beijing will strike back using lethal military power, but there is neither history nor current force-structure to suggest they would ever go abroad in search of foreign conquests. And while they have greatly expanded economic engagement with the world (through programs such as the Belt-and-Road Initiative), they have not built the sea and air transport infrastructure necessary to project meaningful combat power.

Meaning, the most rational policy the U.S. could use on China would be to vigorously compete on economic terms, hold them accountable on trade and intellectual property rights, and maintain a naval and air presence in the Asia-Pacific region to reassure our allies. Pressing military power closer to their borders and conducting frequent so-called "freedom of navigation" operations near Chinese shores, however, is not in America's interests. Provocative military operations do not deter China and will not improve our economic or security posture there.

China is quickly emerging as one of the 2020 election's hottest and most contentious foreign policy issues. Trying to find domestic political advantage by inflating the Beijing threat, however, risks harming American interests.

It is entirely appropriate that we should pay close attention to some of the genuinely troubling behaviors and actions taken by China and apply remedial action where appropriate. Going too far, however, risks causing unnecessary harm to our economy. For all the legitimate challenges that exist in our relations with China, a healthy Sino-American relationship can have distinct and substantive advantages for our country.

China is the third-largest export market for U.S. goods ($120 billion a year) and the largest source of U.S. imports ($540 billion a year), contributing in both directions to a healthy American economy. If handled well, we can cooperate with China in areas of mutual benefit, including reducing global terrorism, improving their human rights record at home and abroad, and in moving towards regional security and cooperation in the Asia-Pacific region. But both the Republicans and Democrats seem intent on using China as a bat with which to beat each other as we get closer to Election Day.

The net results of these back-and-forth broadsides have been to create an anti-China sentiment on both the left and right in America. If the two camps don't get these attacks under control, we risk unnecessarily turning China into an enemy, which will ultimately harm our interests well beyond November's election.

In May 2020, Ambassador Chas Freeman, former deputy director of Mission of the U.S. Embassy in Beijing, told a Harvard audience that relations between Washington and Beijing have unequivocally soured in recent years. Our bilateral relations, he said, have gone from an escalating trade war "to a technology war and from that to political warfare and a rising danger of military strife." U.S.-China relations, he said, "are arguably in the most dangerous state since the Korean War."

These deteriorating conditions are unforced errors and wholly unnecessary, even in the current environment. None of those emotional issues should inform U.S. policy towards China. A cold, hard assessment of our interests should.

For many years now we have done ourselves no favors in demonizing villains abroad—be it China or others—for domestic political advantage, often viewing actors in black-and-white terms. Most nations are a combination of good and bad, but virtually all of them behave more or less predictably according to their definition of what is in the best interests of their countries. We should do the same.

In those areas where we have legitimate disputes with China, we should press the matter to the extent necessary to improve our position. In those areas where we have common cause with China, we should be willing to work with them, especially in the economic sphere. Where we have irreconcilable differences, we should firmly but diplomatically take whatever action is necessary to resolve the matter.

What good would it do our citizens to demonize China to the point that we lose business with them and harm our economy—or worse—see relations deteriorate to the point that one day we come to blows and risk a catastrophically injurious war?

We should, by all means, preserve the security of the U.S. and deter any nation or group from threatening to attack us or taking advantage of our people. We must be wise, however, in how we balance the need for security and the requirement of taking risks to expand economic markets. Going too far in either direction risks losing both.

North Korea:

Kim Jong-un <u>does not want</u> to go to war with the United States. He has no intention of ever using his arsenal in an offensive strike against the U.S. or any of our allies. What he does desire, above all, is to <u>preserve his regime</u> and continue to rule in Pyongyang unchallenged. To accomplish these objectives, Kim seeks to formally end the Korean war, achieve closer political and economic ties with South Korea, and to see his domestic economy expand. All of this gives us an enormous opportunity to ensure security on the peninsula and reduce the risk of war.

We should support South Korea President Moon Jae in his efforts to establish and expand ties with North Korea, work on joint economic development between the two countries, and sign an end-of-war declaration with his neighbor to the north. Anything that reduces the tensions between the two countries and lessens the chance of war is something we should pursue.

The balance of power between the U.S/Republic of Korea alliance and North Korea is so strong toward our side that there is no genuine military or economic competition. Kim likely has a small stockpile of nuclear weapons and does have potent conventional forces, but it is not a fraction of the power Washington and Seoul can bring to bear in the event of war—and Kim knows this better than anyone.

The North Korean nuclear arsenal is expressly designed <u>to deter the United States</u> from attacking him, regime-change style (more on that below)—not to launch a surprise attack against the U.S. His reluctance to attack America has nothing to do with any sense of morality, but out of the absolute certainty that he would be incinerated within 30 minutes.

Thus, Kim is already successfully deterred and there would be no reason for us to ever use so-called "preventative" military strikes to prevent him from attacking. Our security is already guaranteed by our standard nuclear and conventional forces. The best course of action would be to minimize friction and lower the tensions between North and South Korea to preserve the security of all. That is contrasted with U.S. policy of the past several decades, however, which has *never* produced peace and always keeps the threats of war at the fore.

The current policy is to <u>demand full denuclearization</u> upfront as a basis for working towards a peace agreement. Regardless of how much we all wish it weren't so, the fact is that Pyongyang *has* nuclear weapons. No amount of coercion or threats of preemptive war is going to force them to give up their one powerful deterrent card. Trying to force that outcome guarantees failure and keeps alive the risk of stumbling into war.

What is very much possible, however, is a diplomatic and political step-by-step move towards peace with North Korea. The best way to ensure our security is to facilitate reconciliation between South and North Korea, reduce tensions so no party feels threatened, and over time work toward disarmament. Countries that are making economic progress and improving the lives of their people are the least likely to start a war.

Iran:

The Iranian regime and Washington have despised each other since the 1979 revolution when the mullahs took hundreds of Americans hostage. Animosity between our staunchest Middle Eastern ally, Israel, and Iran have also been high. But emotions aside, Iran does not represent a security threat to the U.S. that can't be deterred with our normal nuclear and conventional military posture.

In 2015, President Obama negotiated a deal with Teheran called the <u>Joint Comprehensive Plan of Action</u> that would curtail Iran's ability to make a bomb in exchange for lessening of sanctions and expanded economic opportunities abroad. There was much merit in the deal, especially as it made it less likely Iran could someday produce a nuclear bomb, but it had significant flaws.

The plan didn't include Iran's ballistic missile program and it didn't allow international inspectors to have complete and unfettered access.

But it was <u>so intrusive</u> from the perspective of the Iranian hardliners, that it took considerable effort from their president to convince the government to back it. Once Trump unilaterally canceled the deal in May 2018 and began openly threatening Iran, the <u>hardliners in Iran</u> were emboldened and began pushing back hard.

From their point of view, the West in general did not live up to their side of the deal and betrayed Teheran. When the U.S. pulled out of the deal, Washington imposed severe sanctions that only got harder over time, eventually including almost the complete shut-down of Iranian oil sales. Deprived of that income, the Iranian economy went into free-fall.

Without the constraints of the nuclear deal, Iranian hardliners felt free to ignore key terms of it. Increasingly desperate, they began engaging in riskier behavior in the region, temporarily detaining ships in the Straits of Hormuz and shooting down a U.S. drone they claimed went over its territory (a charge our government denied). Early in 2020, the U.S. and Iran came to the brink of war when the U.S. military <u>killed Iran's</u> senior ranking military officer. In retaliation, Iran launched <u>a rocket attack</u> against a U.S. base in Iraq.

Fortunately, no Americans were killed in Iran's counter-strike and the situation calmed in the weeks that followed. The danger isn't over, however, as we continue to maintain sanctions that strangle the Iranian economy. They continue seeking revenge for the loss of their general, and in September 2020 were accused of plotting to kill an American ambassador. <u>Trump fired back</u>, saying the U.S. would respond to any attack "one-thousand times greater in magnitude."

The question that must be answered by American policymakers, however, is what course of action gives us the best chance at ensuring the security of our military personnel and prosperity of our countrymen. The current, "maximum pressure" campaign – claimed by its supporters to be a tool that would force Iran into compliance to our demands – has done the opposite: it has forced Iran into taking increasingly rash and provocative actions, increased their nuclear activities, and made it easier—not harder—for them to build a bomb should they want to try.

Our policy towards Iran should change and be based on the reality that we don't need to risk war with Iran to preserve American security. Our military is orders of magnitude more powerful than Teheran's. Our Navy and Air Force could, by themselves, sink virtually every boat in Iran's fleet and destroy their jets on the ground or in the air. They would be powerless to stop us from sending missiles to destroy any target in their country – and they know those facts better than anyone.

They would thus never risk an unprovoked attack they know for certainty would destroy most of their armed forces because — similar to the North Korean — they desire to remain in power and would not risk losing the assets that keep them alive.

Moreover, Iran is no threat to become the regional hegemon that many experts laughably warn against. They are more than balanced by regional powers that are ideologically and religiously opposed to them: Saudi Arabia, the Emirates, Egypt, and the most powerful military force in the region, Israel. At best, Iran can balance the powers arrayed against them; there is zero chance they could overpower them.

It makes the most sense, then, to let the countries in the region, with the most to lose from a powerful Iran, take the lead on containing any threat that may one day arise. We should keep our military out of range of Iranian weapons – meaning a withdraw of our troops from both Iraq and Syria. Doing so would greatly constrain their ability to target American military personnel – but they would not be safe from our unrivaled ability to project power anywhere in their country.

We should then rely on diplomacy to negotiate a new, sustainable deal with Iran. But that would mean doing something that we have up to this point been unwilling to contemplate: acknowledge that in any negotiation, both sides have to come out with something they want or there will not be a deal and the risk of escalation and war will remain.

Most in the status quo political establishment reflexively reject any outcome that results in something besides Iranian submission to all Western demands. The hard reality is, it doesn't matter how much we don't like someone or how distasteful it is if they come out of it with something they consider good. Our negotiators have offered little more in the past several years than an undisguised demand of unconditional surrender to the regime in Teheran.

That behavior guarantees diplomatic failure, assures Iran will continue to engage in increasingly risky behavior and keeps the chances of stumbling into a destructive war very high. That is the polar opposite of improving our security and facilitating our prosperity. Constructive realism leads us to take the messy world as it is and make policy that gives us the best chance at achieving outcomes beneficial to Americans, even if it means engaging regimes we don't like. We do it all the time already.

We used to be the most vicious of enemies with Vietnam and yet today we do business with them (even though their form of government is the same as when we lost the Vietnam war). We do business where it benefits us with Saudi Arabia, despite the fact their country engages in all sorts of behavior we otherwise detest.

It is time we stopped trying for unrealistic policies that can't succeed and instead make the best of the messy world we have.

When talking about concepts that should undergird an effective foreign policy, there is one other significant point that I think needs to be addressed, and which both parties have gotten wrong to the detriment of the nation: the deterioration in our adherence to the U.S. Constitution.

No More Unconstitutional Use of Force:

Article I of the Constitution unequivocally declares war-making power belongs in the hands of Congress alone. The 1973 War Powers Act reinforces this. Yet every president of the modern era has ignored this provision of American law and used the military almost as a personal force to be employed wherever his fancy led. That has always been a violation of U.S. law but has become so common that it barely registers on the public radar.

Wars are supposed to be hard to get into, not easy. Obeying the law won't make us any less secure (it won't "tie the hands of the president" as so many falsely claim), it will make us far *more* secure. The Constitution and existing law already give the president the authority to respond to attacks or looming assaults without having to get Congressional authority.

If we followed the law and required that any military action contemplated abroad have Congressional authorization *first*, we'd be far less likely to engage in pointless or unnecessary actions. That would, admittedly, *constrain* the hands of any president to use lethal military action that could suck us into a war our citizens may not think is worth the cost.

That gets at the heart of what our country was founded on: that the government is by the people, for the people, and of the people: it is not the plaything of an unaccountable sovereign. Too often, leaders have considered themselves smarter than the regular people in our country and convinced themselves that if they had to get permission from the people before taking action, the citizens would not "get it" and that would prevent the president from taking his or her preferred action.

But that's not the way our country is supposed to work. The president, the Congress, and the appointed leaders are designed to be *servants* of the people, not regents to rule irrespective of them. The fact is, if leaders cannot convince the people that a given situation warrants the risk of war, then no action should be taken. Period.

It's worth repeating: it is *supposed* to be hard to take the country into war. In cases where there is a genuine threat to our security, any president should be able to make that case to the people, and if the case is strong enough, Congress will authorize the action. It bears repeating: following the law and Constitution will continue to give the president all the power and authorization he or she needs to respond to any actual or imminent attack.

The reason we have our world-class, dominating military is to deter others from attacking us and in ensuring that if any does try, we will crush them. We don't have a powerful military, however, so we can use it all the time. To the contrary, we should use the armed forces infrequently, choosing instead to use our diplomatic skill—backed up by a powerful military—to keep us safe.

That is how you create and maintain a strong nation, a peaceful world, and a prosperous economy.

Conclusion

Whether Donald Trump is sworn in for a second term on Jan. 20, 2021 or Joe Biden is inaugurated, the next president will enter office with a bevy of foreign policy challenges that would put a strain on the most diplomatically astute leader.

The winner will enter 2021 as the one responsible for handling a foreign policy based on antagonist relationships with major powers Russia and China. One that sees us constantly threatening military action against Iran, North Korea, Venezuela, and in which our leaders have increased a war of words against even tiny Cuba.

Our diplomatic actions have resulted in constant friction with the best of our allies in NATO, South Korea, and others in Asia. We have active combat or combat support missions of various sizes ongoing in Syria, Iraq, Afghanistan, Niger, Somalia, Yemen, Libya, and others in Africa. We have scores of sanctions on individuals and regimes currently in place, some of which even target our European friends.

Everywhere one looks, our international relations are fraught with risk and heavily weighted on the use or threat of military action or on coercive measures aimed at bending others to our will. And what have been the results of these strongarm tactics?

Almost complete failure.

After the initial response to the 9/11 terrorist attacks when Bush sent the military into Afghanistan on a limited and attainable military mission, virtually every other military foray into which we've deployed our troops has utterly failed to accomplish their intended purpose.

Yet at the same time, our leaders constantly tell us that the security environment is getting worse and worse. At what point will our leaders see what ought to be the obvious connection between our barely-restrained deployment of force throughout the globe and the deteriorating level of security we enjoy?

The two are unquestionably connected. When we maintain an elevated use of force as the primary means in which we engage the world, when our first response is to threaten or attack those with whom we disagree, we perversely create the very instability we want our military to alleviate.

What the next president needs to do, then, is to recognize this painful reality, stop doing the things that don't make sense—stop blindly repeating the strategies and tactics that have so consistently failed—and form new policies that take the world as it is. He should adopt constructive realism as his guiding philosophy and use effective diplomacy to create the conditions that will best ensure our nation's national security and economic prosperity well into the future.

The next president needs to be clear on one thing: there is no easy way to fix what's been broken. Every individual foreign policy issue at play involves typically multiple, usually divergent, interests, each trying to pull its own way. Creating the best outcome possible for our country involves wise engagement with both adversaries and friends, understanding the motivations and culture of each, and being willing to make principled compromises where necessary to extract the best outcome for our population.

There are no guarantees that we will win in each and every negotiation, but we can be very confident that if the next president enacts a viable, reality-based foreign policy, our country will come out on top more often than not. Even a partial setback, if handled deftly—and with patience—can result in a long-term gain for America.

One other thing I can come close to guaranteeing: if America retains our current status quo foreign policy, if we refuse to end forever-wars, and if we fail to adopt new ways of thinking in how we engage with the world, we will fail.

That could mean anything from being bled dry in pointless military adventures, stumbling into unnecessary real wars that gash our armed forces, or that we suffer preventable economic loss with some of the world's largest trading partners.

The choice is the next Commander-in-Chief's to make. He can refuse to make changes that are obviously necessary and cling to the status quo or adapt our foreign and military policies to a new way, tethered to ground-truth reality. One way leads to almost certain loss and the other leads to potentially great gain.

I hope he chooses well.

Epilogue

Black Swans.

Both our current foreign policy and the one advocated here are predicated on an understanding of the world as we have known it to be for the past few decades. Meaning, the people in most countries—friends and adversaries alike—acknowledge that the world generally revolves around the following realities:

> The U.S. has the most powerful conventional military in the world, has an unrivaled ability to project power globally, and possesses enough nuclear weapons to wipe out half the planet.

> Russia and China are our two biggest competitors and potential adversaries of Western powers, each with meaningful arsenals of nuclear weapons (Russia has an improving, but still limited conventional capability, while China is emerging as a robust but regional conventional power).

> North Korea and Iran represent the next level of potential aggressors, but both have limited military means and anemic economies.

> Europe and other countries in Asia are strong economically, but of average military capabilities, and in any case, don't represent a threat to any nation.

> Africa and South America do not possess a meaningful military arsenal.

Most states operate with the knowledge that since the end of World War II, the U.S. has enjoyed a virtual monopoly on the technology of war, perpetually fielding the best in air, land, and sea platforms and dominates in space. The belief that attacking America would result in a near-certain military defeat is one of the main reasons no nation has attacked us in the past 70 years.

We in the United States, especially among those in our armed forces, believe we will always have a military advantage over all potential adversaries. This certainty has resulted in a quiet but meaningful arrogance within us.

In the many debates in think-tanks and academic settings or in computer war games conducted, the entry point for discussions of conventional war is almost always the same: the U.S. would win in any fight. The questions have revolved around the ease or difficulty of the win, whether we would suffer serious losses on the way to victory or whether it would be a sweeping Desert-Storm style blitz. But is that a safe assumption to make?

Before World War II, the French were the undisputed military masters of the European continent. No one doubted it. Not the Russians, not the Germans, and not the French. They had won World War I and during the two-decade interwar period, the French had prided themselves on experimenting with new technologies and fighting doctrines.

Many in the French armed forces had always believed a fight with Germany would inevitably come and expected at some point Hitler's troops would attack. But they were incredibly confident that they had the best plans, the best equipment, and the best-trained troops so that when Germany did attack, the French would win. May 1940 shattered those assumptions with lightning speed.

The Wehrmacht attacked in ways the French and British allies never expected, with a doctrine for which they were utterly unprepared, and at a speed they had not imagined possible. The combined British and French armies were eviscerated, and the war was lost in less than two weeks. What happened was something of a "black swan" event.

In general terms, a black swan event occurs when something happens to a society or country that dramatically violates what they previously believed to be the left and right parameters of the possible. Sometimes black swans come in the form of acts of nature (such as Hurricane Katrina that destroyed the levees in New Orleans in 2005). Other times they are unexpected reactions to otherwise commonly known systems (the stock market crash of 1929). But they could also happen in the field of armed conflict.

We must keep a healthy degree of humility in all our plans and projections of the future, recognizing that a previously unknown factor could suddenly materialize that dramatically changes all our calculations. For example, we think we have a very good idea of the parameters of the military capabilities Beijing can put in the field and how we can counter or defeat each. But is that a safe bet?

In a 2004 book on Chinese military theory, author Jason E. Bruzdzinski explained that since the mid-1980s, Chinese military experts, "have been studying trends in the development of U.S. defense policy and strategy, operational doctrine, and the enhancement of overall combat capability of the U.S. armed forces." The purpose, he said, was to find new ways to defeat American military units by something called "assassin's mace."

Assassin's mace is not merely a secret new Chinese weapon, but a concept that combines linking a system of weapons together with unexpected or never-before-used doctrine or tactics. Virtually every American weapon system—existing or in development—can be found in the public domain.

Such details are frequently provided via the Government Accountability Office, in which any Chinese person with internet access can read about it. (GAO provided, for example, extensive coverage of the FCS program throughout its development.) The Chinese, in stark contrast, provide very little public information on their weapon systems development.

This dynamic would put the U.S. at a distinct disadvantage should we fight a war against each other, because they would know far more about us than we know about them. It's not that we would be in total darkness; the U.S. has a fairly robust knowledge of Chinese military capabilities.

The Pentagon, for example, annually publishes an analysis of Chinese military capabilities. The <u>2020 report</u> details how China has been developing long-range "carrier-killer" missiles, the ability to blind or destroy our satellites, and that they have an increasingly effective ballistic missile capability. These advances alone will ensure any all-out conventional war between the U.S. and China will be an incredible challenge whose end would not necessarily result in an American win.

But if the Chinese have discovered a way to coordinate these capabilities in tandem with its rapidly modernizing air, land, and sea forces, it could combine the physical weapons of war with new tactics or fighting doctrine that we have never faced nor considered. That could give them an enormous advantage in the early phase of a war—an advantage that could prove decisive to our detriment.

Keep in mind that China has had almost *three decades* to watch, meticulously record, and wargame every aspect of the American way of war. Some of their experts know how we fight better than some U.S. military experts. They have then been able to imagine, conceive, and experiment their new ways of fighting against our known skills and capabilities.

If a war broke out, they would be intellectually experienced at facing off against our known capabilities by using their new 'assassin's mace' weapons and concepts. We, on the other hand, would be having to discover their new doctrine only while on the receiving end of their bombs, missiles, and electronic-warfare attacks.

Coming up with effective countermeasures while suffering the heat of combat is a difficult thing. It took the Western allies upwards of two years before we were able to effectively counter Nazi Germany's "blitzkrieg" concepts. We may not have two years to recover before a war with China in the Asia Pacific could be over.

Whether we're talking about a high-tech war with China, an unexpected fight with Russia in Central or Eastern Europe, or a second Korean war, our policymakers and senior military leaders must remain aware—and not merely in periodic thinking—of the potential for our adversaries to suddenly emerge with black swan capabilities that could deal a severe blow to our forces.

That's not to say we should not be afraid of anyone. We should, however, think very carefully before choosing to fight a war. Today we suffer too much hubris in the unquestioned belief that we will always win every war. Such thinking leads to careless or insufficient diplomatic activity, believing there is little risk to us in simply issuing ultimatums or demands of our adversaries.

Firm preparation, on the other hand, coupled with thorough and informed diplomacy—along with a healthy dose of humility—can keep America strong, free, and prosperous indefinitely.

Made in the USA
Columbia, SC
16 July 2021